W9-CMZ-433

# EAGLES
# ESSENTIAL

Everything You Need to Know
to Be a Real Fan!

Thom Loverro

TRIUMPH
**BOOKS**
CHICAGO

Library of Congress Cataloging-in-Publication Data

Loverro, Thom.
    Eagles essential : everything you need to know to be a real fan !/ Thom Loverro.
    p. cm.
    Includes bibliographical references.
    ISBN-13: 978-1-57243-886-6
    ISBN-10: 1-57243-886-X
    1. Philadelphia Eagles (Football team)—History. 2. Philadelphia Eagles (Football team)—Miscellanea. I. Title.

GV956.P44L68 2006
796.332′640974811—dc22

2006010389

This book is available in quantity at special discounts for your group or organization. For further information, contact:

**Triumph Books**
542 South Dearborn Street
Suite 750
Chicago, Illinois 60605
(312) 939-3330
Fax (312) 663-3557

Printed in U.S.A.
ISBN-13: 978-1-57243-886-6
ISBN-10: 1-57243-886-X
Design by Patricia Frey
All photos courtesy of Rusty Kennedy except where otherwise indicated

# Contents

The Yellow Jackets Buzz ........................................... 1

The Eagle Flies .................................................. 7

A Jailbird and a Star: Alabama Pitts ............................ 13

The Early Years ................................................. 18

Bell's Vision ................................................... 23

Trading Teams ................................................... 30

A Football Innovator: Greasy Neale ............................. 36

The Steagles Take the Stage ..................................... 41

"Wham Bam" Van Buren Takes the Eagles to the Top ............ 46

Titletown I ..................................................... 50

Titletown II .................................................... 54

Concrete Charlie: The Incomparable Chuck Bednarik ........... 59

The Lean Years .................................................. 63

Champions ....................................................... 69

Tommy McDonald: A Showman and a Star ....................... 74

The Abyss ....................................................... 79

A Familiar Pattern . . . . . . . . . . . . . . . . . . . . . . . . . . . . . . . . . . 86

Promises of a Super Bowl: The Arrival of Dick Vermeil . . . . . . . . . 92

The Polish Rifle Comes to Philly: Ron Jaworski Joins the Eagles . . . . 97

The Road to the Super Bowl . . . . . . . . . . . . . . . . . . . . . . . . . . . 102

Burnout . . . . . . . . . . . . . . . . . . . . . . . . . . . . . . . . . . . . . . . . . . 108

"Bud-dee, Bud-dee" . . . . . . . . . . . . . . . . . . . . . . . . . . . . . . . . . . 114

Head Coach Changes: Ryan to Kotite . . . . . . . . . . . . . . . . . . . . 120

A Milestone on the Sidelines . . . . . . . . . . . . . . . . . . . . . . . . . . 125

A Championship Pedigree . . . . . . . . . . . . . . . . . . . . . . . . . . . . 130

When McNabb Touched Down . . . . . . . . . . . . . . . . . . . . . . . . . 137

Missing Link Found? . . . . . . . . . . . . . . . . . . . . . . . . . . . . . . . . 142

As the World Turns . . . . . . . . . . . . . . . . . . . . . . . . . . . . . . . . . . 149

Not Even Santa Is Safe . . . . . . . . . . . . . . . . . . . . . . . . . . . . . . . 155

Answers to Trivia Questions . . . . . . . . . . . . . . . . . . . . . . . . . . . 160

Philadelphia Eagles All-Time Roster . . . . . . . . . . . . . . . . . . . . . 162

Notes . . . . . . . . . . . . . . . . . . . . . . . . . . . . . . . . . . . . . . . . . . . . 183

# The Yellow Jackets Buzz

The roots of the Philadelphia Eagles were planted in a northeast neighborhood known as Frankford in 1899. It began when a group of men met to form the Frankford Athletic Association. This was a time when neighborhoods formed social clubs and athletic clubs for socializing. The association started with a baseball team but later added soccer and then football. It was hardly sandlot competition, however. These clubs fielded competitive teams. In the year of its creation, the Frankford football team defeated the Philadelphia Athletic Club, Jefferson Medical College, and, in its biggest game of the year, on Thanksgiving Day before a crowd of about 2,000 spectators, the Philadelphia & Reading YMCA by a score of 28–0.

Records show that the Frankford Athletic Association disbanded about 10 years later. Some members went on to form the Loyola Athletic Club and then, several years later, re-formed the Frankford Athletic Association. The Frankford football team, known as the Yellow Jackets, became one of the region's top teams.

At the same time, professional football had been taking root in the Philadelphia area as well. In 1902 baseball's Philadelphia Athletics, managed by Connie Mack, and the Philadelphia Phillies formed their own professional football teams then joined with the Pittsburgh Stars in the first attempt at a pro football league. They called it the National Football League. It would not last, but another organization—called the American Professional Football Association (APFA)—formed in 1920 as more professional football teams sprang up in the Northeast and Midwest. Two years later the APFA changed its name to the one previously used by the professional teams from Philadelphia and became the National Football League.

**DID YOU KNOW ...** That the Frankford Yellow Jackets were not allowed to play football on Sundays because of Pennsylvania's blue laws? But that didn't stop them from playing. They played home games on Saturday nights. Usually they would then get on a train with the team they had just played in order to have another game somewhere else on Sunday. This is why Frankford often wound up playing more games each season than any other team in the NFL.

Semipro and so-called amateur football clubs were growing in popularity along with pro football teams, and amateurs and pros sometimes met in exhibition games. Frankford played a number of professional teams and more than held their own, compiling a 6–2–1 record over two years and playing the NFL champions of 1922, the Canton Bulldogs, in a 3–0 loss. By 1924 the Frankford Athletic Association's team, playing at a field that held about 10,000 fans, was ready to join the NFL. It had a successful 1924 debut, defeating the Rochester Jeffersons 21–0. The Yellow Jackets played 14 league games that year, more than any other team, and posted an 11–2–1 mark. However, even though they won more games than the Cleveland Bulldogs (7–1–1) or the Chicago Bears (6–1–4), they finished third behind those teams in the league standings, which were compiled according to winning percentage, not number of victories. As long as a team played in the league's minimum number of games, they qualified, as the Bulldogs (whose only loss had been to the Yellow Jackets) and the Bears did.

During the eight years in which the Frankford team was a part of this version of the NFL, they played more league games than any other franchise. Most of the team's home games during that period were played on Saturdays—a day usually reserved for college football—because the Yellow Jackets were hampered by Pennsylvania's blue laws, which prohibited such activities on Sundays so they would not interfere with religious observations and services. Away games, however, could still be played on Sundays.

The coach of the first-place Cleveland team that beat out the Yellow Jackets in 1924 was Guy Chamberlin, a legendary former All-American from the University of Nebraska who had been a player/coach on NFL championship teams in Canton in 1922 and 1923. In 1914, his junior year, he returned a kickoff 95 yards and ran 70 yards from scrimmage for a touchdown. In 1915, his senior year, Nebraska upset Notre Dame 20–19, thanks in large part to Chamberlin, who scored the Cornhuskers' first two touchdowns on runs of 20 and 10 yards and then completed two passes for 49 yards and the winning touchdown. He played for the independent Canton Bulldogs in 1919 and the Decatur Staleys, with player/coach George Halas, the following season. In 1920 Chamberlin ran back two long interceptions for the Staleys, one for 70 yards and another for 75.

Chamberlin came to coach and play for the Yellow Jackets in 1925 and played 20 league games in a year when the team had a 13–7 record. One of those games was part of the legendary Chicago Bears–Red Grange tour that is often credited with helping to put pro football on the map. On December 5 at Shibe Park an estimated crowd of 35,000 watched as the Yellow Jackets lost 14–7 to the Bears in the rain. Grange scored both touchdowns in a game in which the final two quarters were shortened because of darkness.

The 1925 Yellow Jackets would also play a role in one of the most disputed controversies in the history of the league. The Pottsville Maroons had come to Philadelphia to play an exhibition game against the Notre Dame All-Stars. It was seen by league president Joe Carr as an invasion of Frankford's territorial rights, and he prohibited the game. The team from Pottsville played it anyway, and Carr suspended the Maroons, who were considered by many to be the best team in the league in 1925. Because of the suspension, the heralded Maroons did not qualify for the official league championship, which was won that year by the Chicago Cardinals.

There was much optimism and interest in the Yellow Jackets after the 1925 season, not only because of Chamberlin, but also because of other players who were becoming fan favorites. One such player was "Two Bits" Homan, otherwise known as Babe Homan—perhaps the smallest player in NFL history at 5'5" and weighing only 145 pounds. Frankford tackle Russell "Bull" Behman, who played against Homan in college, advised the Yellow Jackets to take a chance on the diminutive player—and it was a chance that paid off. Homan was a star punt returner for the Yellow Jackets from 1925 to 1930 and averaged nearly 14 yards a return on 82 returns. He was also a star defensive back, intercepting five passes in his first two seasons with Frankford. One

Philadelphia sportswriter wrote about Homan's popularity with the football crowds: "Every move Homan makes is colorful. The spectators look for this midget to perform some spectacular feat every time he takes a step, whether he has the ball or not."

In 1926 Chamberlin led Frankford to the NFL championship with a record of 14–1–2. The 14 victories set a league record for regular-season wins, a record that lasted until the San Francisco 49ers went 15–1 in 1984. One key game that year came against the Green Bay Packers on Thanksgiving Day. With the Yellow Jackets trailing 14–13 in the fourth quarter, it was Homan who caught a pass and ran 38 yards for the game-winning touchdown. According to *The Philadelphia Inquirer,* Homan's game-winning score resulted in "a spectacle of joyful exuberance not witnessed in this [the] professional gridiron annals in this dear Quaker city of ours. Oh, what a bedlam, as hats and other miscellaneous articles were tossed in the air, and the crowd threatened to break forth in its demonstration in true rabble fashion on the gridiron."

Two Bits certainly was a crowd pleaser.

Another key game that year was the season finale, played against the Pottsville Maroons, who were allowed back in the league to prevent them from joining the rival American Football League (AFL). They came into the game with a 10–2–1 record. More than 8,000 fans showed up on a frigid December day at Yellow Jacket Field to watch the two teams battle to a scoreless tie.

The game considered to be the championship contest that year took place at Shibe Park against the Chicago Bears, who had beaten Frankford the last three times they played by a combined score of 66–10. This time would be different, though. Yellow Jackets quarterback Houston Stockton threw a touchdown pass to Homan for a 7–6 Frankford win and Chamberlin's fourth championship in five years with three different franchises. Chamberlin delivered the game's key play by blocking the Bears' extra point, preserving the one-point margin of victory.

Chamberlin would depart the following year, leaving the Frankford organization in disarray. The Yellow Jackets turned to tackle Ed Weir for help. Weir was a two-time All American from the University of Nebraska and one of the greatest players to come out of that school in the early days of its football program. Once, after a Notre Dame–Nebraska contest, Notre Dame coach Knute Rockne visited Weir in the Nebraska

Huskers locker room to compliment him, calling him "one of the greatest tackles" he had ever seen. Weir would later be inducted into the College Football Hall of Fame. He came to play for Frankford in 1926, then took over for Chamberlin as player/coach in 1927.

The Yellow Jackets recorded their first losing season that year, going 6–9–3, but finished with a winning record in their last 10 games (4–4–2), showing some promise for the season to come. Weir brought Frankford back to its winning ways in 1928 with a record of 11–3–2, but the team finished second in the NFL standings behind the Providence Steam Rollers—even though the Yellow Jackets had played five more games and had three more wins than Providence had. The Steam Rollers had the better winning percentage, putting them on top according to league rules.

The next coaching change took place in 1929 as another Frankford player, "Bull" Behman, took the reins. Behman's size (5'10", 230 pounds) and reportedly quick movements let him become one of the NFL's top linemen in the 1920s. He had been a star lineman at Dickinson College and came to play for the Yellow Jackets in 1924. He was also a place-kicker and had kicked a number of game-winning field goals for Frankford, including one in 1925 that gave the Yellow Jackets a 5–3 victory over the New York Giants. *The Philadelphia Inquirer* described Behman's victorious kick as follows: "In the clever and deadly toe of Captain Behman, victory lurked for the Yellow Jackets—everybody realized that the kick had snatched victory from the very jaws of defeat, that a certain New York victory had been transmuted by Behman's magic alchemy into a Hornet triumph."

Behman left Frankford in 1926 to play for the Philadelphia Quakers in the new American Football League and became captain of that squad. That league folded after one season, however, and in 1927 Behman came back to the Yellow Jackets. Two years later he became player/coach for Frankford, posting a respectable 10–4–5 record, good enough for a third-place finish.

Frankford had now established a tradition as one of the better football teams in the league and had hopes of being part of the NFL for years to come.

## TRIVIA

**Why were the Pottsville Maroons, one of Frankford's chief rivals, suspended from the league in 1925?**

*Answers to the trivia questions are on pages 160–161.*

But the Great Depression, which was about to take hold all over America, played havoc with the hopes of people across the nation. Many factories and businesses closed in and around the Philadelphia area and support for the team suffered. The Yellow Jackets had difficulty paying good players and fielding a competitive team in 1930, and finished with a 6–13–1 record (4–13–1 in the league). A fire at Yellow Jacket Field forced the club to play their 1931 home games at three different locations. Attendance continued to suffer, so much so that in October, league president Joe Carr declared them a "traveling team" for the remainder of the season, which for the Yellow Jackets ended in November. That was the death knell for the Frankford Yellow Jackets.

The franchise remained dormant until July 8, 1933, when two former college football players led a group of investors who purchased the Yellow Jackets for $2,500 and a payment of 25 percent of the money the Frankford franchise still owed creditors. That new franchise would become the Philadelphia Eagles.

# The Eagle Flies

DeBenneville "Bert" Bell was a Pennsylvania blue blood, born into a powerful and rich Philadelphia family. His grandfather had been a member of Congress, and his father served as attorney general for the state of Pennsylvania.

In addition to politics, the family's other passion was athletics—particularly football. Bell's father worked with the legendary Walter Camp on the committee that created the rules for college football. Bell himself played quarterback for the University of Pennsylvania from 1915 to 1919, only missing play during one year, when he left school to serve in World War I. He fulfilled his military service in France with the 20th General Field Hospital, a mobile unit that had been formed at Penn. After finishing his last year at Penn in 1919, he came back to coach there for nine years and then went on to coach at nearby Temple University for two years.

While playing at Penn, Bell became close to teammate Lud Wray, a lineman who went on to play for the Buffalo Bisons and coach at Penn. In 1932 George Preston Marshall, a friend of NFL founder George Halas, purchased the bankrupt Duluth Eskimos for $100 and moved them to Boston to start an NFL franchise there. He hired Wray to coach the new team, called the Boston Braves. The Braves finished 4–4–2 and suffered an estimated $46,000 in losses.

Marshall was ready to fire Wray after the first season, but the coach had his own plans. He had been talking to his former teammate Bell about becoming partners in their own NFL franchise—buying the defunct Frankford Yellow Jackets with a group that included former Philadelphia Phillies executive Jack Potter and Fitz Eugene Dixon, a wealthy Main Line Philadelphia businessman. Bell and Wray bought the

7

Frankford franchise for $2,500 along with an agreement to cover some of the debts owed by the bankrupt team.

Although Bell had come from a rich family from the monied area in Pennsylvania known as the Main Line, the family fortune was wiped out by the 1929 stock market crash. So where did the money that started the Philadelphia Eagles come from? A show girl.

The popular actress/comedienne Frances Upton appeared on Broadway in the 1920s and 1930s, appeared in revues, played the Palace Theater in New York, performed in a radio broadcast, and starred in one of the very first experimental television broadcasts.

And so in 1933, the Philadelphia Eagles were born out of Upton's pocketbook and the brains and vision of her husband, Bert Bell.

That year was to be filled with great change throughout the United States and the world. Prohibition was repealed. Franklin D. Roosevelt took office for his first term and began his New Deal program to try to pull the country out of the Great Depression. (In fact, Bell and Wray actually called their new franchise the Philadelphia Eagles because the eagle was the symbol of the New Deal National Recovery Act.) And in Europe, Adolf Hitler took over as chancellor of Germany.

There was a change in the political climate in Pennsylvania as well. The state's blue laws, prohibiting business on Sundays, were seen as a huge obstacle to the success of pro football, which was laying claim to Sunday afternoons all across America. Professional baseball wasn't crazy about the restrictions, either, and Philadelphia Athletics owner Connie Mack lobbied for a change, threatening to move his baseball team across the Delaware River to Camden, New Jersey. As a result Pennsylvania Governor Gifford Pinchot signed a new law allowing Sunday sporting events.

The blue law change resulted in not just one but two new NFL franchises in Pennsylvania. In addition to the Eagles, Art Rooney, a gambler and businessman from Pittsburgh, also came into the league with a new franchise, the Pittsburgh Pirates, later to be known as the Steelers. The fortunes of the Pittsburgh and Philadelphia franchises were tied together for a variety of reasons in the early days of both teams. They would be joined even more closely nine years later, when the two teams would actually merge for a brief period.

One other team—the Cincinnati Reds—joined the NFL in 1933, while the Staten Island franchise folded. The league was divided into two

*NFL Commissioner Bert Bell (seated in center) is pictured with team owners in 1946. He founded the Philadelphia Eagles in 1933.* Photo courtesy of AP/Wide World Photos.

divisions, the East and the West. The East consisted of the Eagles, the Pirates, the New York Giants, the Boston Redskins (George Preston Marshall changed the name from the Braves in 1933), and the Brooklyn Dodgers. The West was made up of the Reds, the Chicago Cardinals, the Chicago Bears, the Portsmouth Spartans, and the Green Bay Packers.

There would be a number of rule changes in 1933, spurred by circumstances surrounding the 1932 NFL championship game (the first of its kind). In 1932 the Portsmouth Spartans tied the Chicago Bears for first place in the league, so the owners decided to hold a game to determine the champion. The game was supposed to be held at the Bears' home, Wrigley Field. But a blizzard and severe cold forced officials to move the December 11 contest indoors to Chicago Stadium, thereby playing the first arena football game as well.

Early Eagles

### The First Official Philadelphia Eagles Roster

**Backs:** Oran Pape, Dick Thornton, Dick Lachman, John Roberts, Thomas "Swede" Hanson, Les Maynard, Lee Woodruff, Nick Prisco, and Henry O'Boyle.

**Ends:** Tony Kostos, Fred Felber, George Kenneally, Henry Obst, and Alex Marcus.

**Centers:** John "Bull" Lipski, Ray Smith, and Art Koeninger.

**Tackles:** Stan Sokolis, Charles "Tex" Leyendecker, Paul Cuba, and Guy Turnbow.

**Guard:** Joe Kresky, Osborne "Diddie" Wilson, Roy Lechthaler, and George Demas.

Chicago Stadium was the home of the National Hockey League's Chicago Blackhawks. It was also used for boxing matches and other events. During the week before the football game, a circus had performed there. In preparation for the football game, the concrete floor was covered with several inches of dirt. Truckloads of dirt, wood shavings, and bark were then piled on top of the dirt to provide more cushioning.

The dimensions of Chicago Stadium meant that some rules had to be changed. The field was only 80 yards long, and it was 30 feet narrower than the standard football field. Additionally, the sidelines butted up against the stands. The short field meant that the goal posts had to be moved from the end lines to the goal lines. The ball was automatically moved back to the 20-yard line every time either team crossed midfield. And for the first time, all plays would start with the ball on or between the hash marks.

Before that time, the league had been playing under collegiate rules—a forward pass from behind the line of scrimmage was not allowed. But in 1933 it opted to adopt most of the new rules created for the 1932 championship game in Chicago. All plays would start with the ball on or between the hash marks. To increase the number of field goals and decrease the number of tie games, the goal posts were moved from the end lines at the back of the end zones to the goal lines. According to the new rules, when a punt hit the opponent's goal posts before being touched by a player of either team, it would be a touchback. It was a safety if a ball kicked behind the goal line hit the goal posts, rolled back out of the end zone, or was recovered by the kicking team

The forward pass was now legal anywhere behind the line of scrimmage. Previously the passer had had to be at least five yards back from the scrimmage line. The change was called the "Bronko Nagurski Rule" after he scored a controversial touchdown in the 1932 title game. With a scoreless tie going into the fourth quarter of that game, Chicago's Carl Brumbaugh handed the ball off to Nagurski, who then threw it to Red Grange in the end zone for the score. The Spartans argued that Nagurski did not drop back the required five yards before passing to Grange, but the touchdown stood, and the Bears later added a safety for the 9–0 win.

The shape of the ball also changed in 1933. The early football had been rounder than the modern ball, which made it difficult to throw a tight spiral to keep it on target over any distance. Passes were often thrown high into the air, more like a shot put than a modern football pass.

It was a new era for the NFL, and the Eagles were a part of it. After holding a training camp at Bader Field, the first official Philadelphia Eagles team was ready to play, and Coach Wray was ready to take the men into battle on the field. He prepared them with a series of exhibition games against professional and semipro clubs. There was reason to be encouraged after the Eagles won six of those games, beating Clifton, Ohio, 6–0; Bridgeport, Connecticut, 13–0; Orange, New Jersey, 14–7; Paterson, New Jersey, 12–0; U.S. Marines, 40–0; and, appropriately, a semipro team from Frankford called the Legion, 40–0.

The Legion was one of several semipro teams that played in Frankford and joined the Interstate Professional Football League in 1932. They played their home games on a portion of the old Yellow Jacket Field. In 1933, as the memory of the Frankford

# TRIVIA

**By 1934, how many small-town teams remained in the NFL?**

*Answers to the trivia questions are on pages 160–161.*

11

**DID YOU KNOW . . .** That one of the original investors in the Philadelphia Eagles was a wealthy businessman named Fitz Eugene Dixon? Years later his son would also become a sports franchise owner: Fitz Eugene Dixon Jr. owned the Philadelphia 76ers from 1976 to 1981.

Yellow Jackets began to fade and the presence of the Philadelphia Eagles began to take shape, the Legion changed its name to the Yellow Trojans and their stadium was renamed Yellow Trojans Athletic Field.

With the Eagles' only exhibition loss coming in a hard-fought game at the hands of a former NFL franchise—the Staten Island Stapletons, who beat the Eagles 7–0—there was a lot of optimism over the franchise's inaugural season prospects.

Then the exhibition season was over and the games that counted started, and that optimism soon disappeared.

# A Jailbird and a Star: Alabama Pitts

There have been many characters who have donned the uniform of the Philadelphia Eagles over the history of the franchise. But perhaps none had a better story and created more attention during such a brief stay than Edwin "Alabama" Pitts, who signed a $1,500 contract to play for the Eagles in 1935.

Pitt was a hardscrabble kid who grew up to become a famous athlete. He was born in Opelika, Alabama, and joined the navy at the age of 15 after both his father and stepfather had died. Shortly after he got out of the military, at age 19, with the country still mired in the Great Depression, Pitts landed in New York broke and without prospects. Using a gun, he and an accomplice robbed a grocery store of reportedly $76.25. They were caught, and Pitts was sentenced to Sing Sing Prison for a term "not less than eight years and no more than 15."

Alabama Pitts found his calling in prison, and it was athletics. The institution had an active athletics program, and Pitts was a standout in football, basketball, baseball, and track. He became a legend on the prison athletic circuit for his skills, and he gained a good deal of attention from the outside world for his play behind bars. Johnny Evers, general manager of the Albany Senators in baseball's International League (and part of the legendary Chicago Cubs infield team of Tinkers to Evers to Chance), signed Pitts to a $200-a-month contract in May 1935, while Pitts was still a month away from being paroled. Because these were tough times for all spectator events, gimmicks—such as pole sitting and other stunts—were used to make money and garner attention. The signing of Pitts was considered by many to be a publicity stunt, particularly because the Senators were in last place and not drawing well.

*Alabama Pitts leaves Sing Sing prison with his mother, Erma Rudd, after serving five years of an eight- to 15-year sentence for armed robbery.* Photo courtesy of Bettmann/CORBIS.

The signing was not well received by International League president Charles H. Knapp, who refused to approve the contract, saying it was not "in the best interests of the game." But by then Pitts had become a sort of national folk hero. The decision was appealed to baseball's National Association Executive Committee, which upheld Knapp's ruling. But Pitts's situation had become front page news, and *The New York Times* editorialized that the decision to keep Pitts out of baseball was "unfortunate in every way. The Association president was wrong in his assumption that the public would resent his inclusion in baseball. It is more likely to resent his exclusion."

The convict became a cause célèbre. People argued about Alabama Pitts all over the country; there was even a report of a store merchant in Otisville, New York, suffering a heart attack during an argument about him. Hollywood entered the picture when filmmaker Hal Roach offered Pitts a job. The former jailbird would even appear on popular singer Kate Smith's radio show.

There was one last hope for Pitts—an appeal to baseball commissioner Judge Kenesaw Mountain Landis, who was considered a hard sell and unlikely to rule in the convict's favor. But Landis surprised many by ruling that Pitts should be allowed to play, but only in games that mattered—a condition designed to keep Albany from using him merely as an exhibition game publicity stunt

Nearly 8,000 fans watched Pitts make his debut on June 23, 1935, against Jersey City, and he did well at first, going 2 for 5. But he couldn't stay healthy; as the season progressed he suffered a shoulder bruise, a sprained finger, and a spike injury that led to blood poisoning. Pitts wound up batting only .233 in 43 games and was a terrible outfielder. But none of that got in the way of his status as a folk hero and media darling.

In Philadelphia, the Eagles were struggling at the gate and owner Bert Bell needed his own media darling. Bell offered Pitts a short-term contract for a remarkable amount of money at the time: $1,500. He would be worth that amount in publicity because, at that time, pro football was still relegated to small newspaper write-ups and had to compete with many other sports for attention. Besides, it took that amount of money to outbid the other teams seeking Pitts's services, Pittsburgh and Brooklyn.

The Eagles had been in training camp for three weeks already when Pitts arrived in Philadelphia on September 10. He was met by reporters and he didn't disappoint, telling them that his weak batting average and fielding problems were due in part to night games, which had just been instituted that season. "You see, where I was, we didn't get out much at night," Pitts joked with the writers. "If any did, it wasn't to play ball."

Reporters loved him, as did Eagles fans—more than 20,000 came for the September 13 opening game against

## TRIVIA

**What is the name of the fictional character who led a prison football team in Robert Altman's film *The Longest Yard*?**

*Answers to the trivia questions are on pages 160–161.*

Pittsburgh. They were disappointed, though, when Pitts, a halfback and defensive back, did not play. The crowd chanted, "We want Pitts. We want Pitts," during the game, which the Eagles lost 17–7. The team traveled to Detroit the following Sunday only to be pummeled by the Lions, 35–0, and again Pitts did not see any action. He did not take the field until a September 26 exhibition game against the Orange Tornadoes, and though he did not distinguish himself as a running back, he showed some promise as a defensive back.

Pitts made his NFL debut on October 9 in Pittsburgh, where he intercepted two passes in a 17–6 win. Eagles fans finally got to see him at home on October 13 in a game against the Chicago Bears. More than 22,000 spectators came to cheer for the prison legend, who caught a 20-yard pass late in the game in a 39–0 beating by the Bears.

But that would be the end of the relationship between Alabama Pitts and the Philadelphia Eagles. His contract was up, and this time Bell was not willing to spend the money to keep him with the team. He offered Pitts $50 a game. "Pitts has a bright future," Bell told reporters. "And we appreciate that he tries all the time and eventually should be a topflight player. But he lacks experience and needs a lot of work."

Pitts declined, saying he would stick with baseball. But he never became more than a mediocre minor league player. He began the 1936 baseball season with Albany, but by April 10 was demoted to the York club in the New York–Pennsylvania League, where he hit only .224. The team moved to Trenton in July, and Pitts was released by the end of the month. He played only 27 games for Winston-Salem in the Piedmont League in 1937 before being let go.

Pitts settled down in Valdese, North Carolina, worked in a mill, married, and began raising a family. He played semipro baseball until 1940, when a minor league franchise called the Rebels was started in

Hickory in the Tar Heel League. This time Pitts put up very respectable numbers, batting .302 with 39 RBI in 64 games. The franchise closed up shop for a season in 1941 when the league disbanded, and Pitts went back to playing semipro ball in Valdese.

This is where the legend of Alabama Pitts takes a tragic but very Hollywood-style turn. As the story goes, after playing a game on June 6, Pitts went to a local dance hall, and after cutting in to dance with a woman, was stabbed by a Mr. Newland LeFevers, the woman's date. Pitts was taken to Valdese General Hospital, where he bled to death. He was declared dead at 5:00 AM on June 7, 1941.

Newspapers from around the country wrote about the remarkable career and shocking death of Alabama Pitts, and fans in Philadelphia who had adopted him as their hero wondered what might have been had fate dealt the jailhouse legend a different hand.

# The Early Years

The first season for any team in any sport is generally a losing proposition, and the 1933 Philadelphia Eagles were no exception. They struggled both on the field and at the box office in their inaugural season, and at times there were doubts that there would even be a second season. Then again, any business venture started in 1933 in America was a huge risk.

The Eagles didn't play their first regular-season NFL game until October 16 in New York against the Giants. At the birth of the franchise, the starting offensive lineup featured quarterback Dick Thornton, running backs John Roberts and Lee Woodruff, fullback John White, ends Joe Carter and George Kenneally, tackles Paul Cuba and Joe Carpe, guards Roy Lechthaler and Joe Kresky, and center Art Koeninger. They weren't exactly a match for the likes of the Giants, a team coached by the legendary Steve Owen and led by great players like future Pro Football Hall of Fame center and linebacker Mel Hein and rookie quarterback sensation Harry Newman out of the University of Michigan. The Giants had already played three league games that season, winning two and losing one, and they crushed Philadelphia 56–0. It would be a rough debut for the Eagles, who, because of the quirks and uncertainties of NFL scheduling in the early days of the league, would host their home opener against another powerful team, the Portsmouth Spartans, who had already beaten the Giants 17–7 themselves.

The Eagles played their home games for the first three years of their existence at the Baker Bowl, which was the home of baseball's Philadelphia Phillies. The facility became the first dual-purpose stadium in the state when the Eagles began playing their games there. The stadium, which seated 18,000, opened in 1887, and the wooden grand-stand was badly damaged in an 1894 fire. Then, at a 1903 doubleheader, the third-base stands collapsed, killing 12 people. It was the last place Babe Ruth, as a Boston Brave, would ever play in the Major Leagues. It was also the place where Woodrow Wilson became the first president to see a World Series game when he attended the second game of the 1915 Series. The stadium also served as the home of many Negro League base-ball games and hosted Negro League World Series games from 1924 to 1926. The Eagles left the facility after 1935. Two years later the Phillies moved to Shibe Park, and in 1950, the Baker Bowl was torn down.

In 1993 more than 5,000 fans showed up at the Baker Bowl for the first Philadelphia Eagles NFL home game, and they saw their team take a 25–0 beating—the second straight game without an Eagles touch-down. Luckily the Eagles would not have to worry about facing the Spartans the following season—at least not in Portsmouth, Ohio. The franchise would fold after the 1933 season and then move to Detroit to become the Lions.

Lud Wray's crew finally got on the board in their third league game of the season, but Philadelphia fans didn't see it. The Eagles scored the franchise's first touchdown in Green Bay during a 35–9 loss to the Packers. The touchdown play was a 35-yard pass from quarterback Roger Kirkman to Swede Hanson.

The Eagles improved the following week in Cincinnati, defeating the Reds 6–0 on a Hanson touchdown following a lateral pass. They came home to a little more optimism than when they left—and also the chance to play on Sunday, as the state legislature had finally passed the amend-ments to the blue laws that allowed Sunday spectator sporting events. Those two developments brought out 18,000 spectators for the Eagles' return home to the Baker Bowl, where they saw a different team than the one that had been manhandled in its first two home games. The Eagles played the legendary Chicago Bears—the team featuring Bronko Nagurski and Red Grange that would go on to win the NFL champi-onship that season—to a 3–3 tie on field goals by Jack Manders for Chicago and Guy Turnbow for Philadelphia.

The Eagles were finally playing like an NFL team; Wray had molded a strong defensive unit. The offense finally broke through in the sixth

DID YOU KNOW . . .

That running back Thomas "Swede" Hanson, from Temple University, was the first Philadelphia Eagle to be named to the All-Pro team, receiving the honor in 1933 and 1934? While Hanson was running wild in Philadelphia, a baby boy named Robert Fort Hanson was born in East Orange, New Jersey, in 1933. He would grow up to become another Swede Hanson—a popular professional wrestler.

game of the year, a 25–6 win over Pittsburgh before a disappointingly small crowd of 6,000. Those who showed up were treated to an offensive show, as Kirkman threw for two touchdowns to Joe Carter—a 15-yarder and a 37-yard scoring pass—and touchdown runs were made by Hanson and Lee Woodruff. The Eagles were now 2–3–1 and had a chance to get to .500 the following week, hosting the team they had beaten for their first win three weeks earlier—the Cincinnati Reds.

It was a combined effort by both the offense and the defense that gave Philadelphia a 20–3 win against the Reds, including touchdown runs by Sylvester "Red" Davis and John Roberts and a 55-yard interception runback by Woodruff. The victory gave the Eagles a 3–3–1 record, bringing them to the .500 mark and sparking hope that they were on their way to becoming one of the more successful teams in the league.

Unfortunately the Eagles lost their last two games that season. But their final game and loss was actually a measure of how far the franchise had come both on and off the field. Playing at home, they drew their largest crowd of the season, with more than 18,000 fans in attendance. They faced the same Giants that had destroyed them 56–0 in their first league game; this time the Eagles achieved a much less lopsided score of 20–14. The Giants would finish the season with an 11–3 record and go on to lose to the Bears in the NFL title game by a score of 23–21.

The final league record for the Eagles in the franchise's inaugural season was 3–5–1, good enough for fourth place in the division. Swede Hanson was the star of the franchise. He led the team in rushing, carrying the ball 133 times for 494 yards and three touchdowns, and he led in receiving as well, pulling down 9 passes for 140 yards and one touchdown. Hanson also led the team on defense with three interceptions. Quarterback Roger Kirkman completed 22 of 73 passes for 354 yards and two touchdowns, but he also had a dismal 13 interceptions.

Going into the second season, the Eagles faced new rule changes for the league that would continue to increase the use of the forward pass. Previously, if a team had an incomplete pass in the end zone, it would lose possession of the ball, no matter what the down was. Now teams could keep the ball until fourth down even if they tried and failed to complete an end zone pass.

The changes would not have much effect on the Eagles, who showed only slight improvement in their second season, going 4–7 and tying for third in the Eastern Division. One of their victories was a 6–0 triumph over the mighty Giants in their final game of the year before a crowd of more than 12,000 at the Baker Bowl. However, the most memorable victory was a remarkable 64–0 beating of the Reds at home, a win that was particularly welcome because it came after Philadelphia had been shut out in its three previous games and had scored only 30 points total in six games. In the win over Cincinnati, Hanson rushed for 190 yards and scored three touchdowns, as did Joe Carter. Sadly, the Reds went out of business after that, finishing the season as the St. Louis Gunners.

One of the Eagles' losses in 1934 was a particularly tough one for Wray and Bell to swallow—a 6–0 defeat by the Boston Redskins. This was the first time the two teams had met since Wray left Boston owner George Preston Marshall after their inaugural 1932 season, and Marshall was a man who knew how to hold a grudge. There was no love lost between him and Wray, who desperately wanted to beat his former owner. This rivalry would be carried on even after Wray had left Philadelphia and the Redskins had moved to Washington, D.C.

Because the Eagles won three of their final five games in 1934—and because of the emergence of Hanson as a star running back, rushing for 805 yards that year and averaging 5.5 yards per carry—there was much optimism that perhaps Philadelphia might be ready to become a winning organization. It was not yet to be. They lost their first two games of the 1935 season 17–7 to Pittsburgh at home and 35–0 to the Lions in Detroit, then turned around and faced Pittsburgh again, this time coming away with a 17–6 victory on the road. They followed that up with two more

## TRIVIA

**Who led the NFL in pass receptions in 1934?**

*Answers to the trivia questions are on pages 160–161.*

losses, but eased their pain somewhat by beating the hated Redskins and Marshall in Boston in a 7–6 victory. It would be Philadelphia's last win of the season and, as it turned out, the last win for Wray as Eagles coach. They went on to lose their final five games, finishing with a 13–6 loss to the Packers before a small home crowd of about 4,000—not surprisingly, their attendance was dropping due to the lack of victories. Not even the attraction of former Sing Sing convict Alabama Pitts on the roster could soften the financial blow. The Eagles finished the 1935 season with a 2–9 record, the worst mark in the league. Bell tried to cut his losses by cutting a key position: coach. Dismissing Wray, Bell made himself the team's head coach.

# Bell's Vision

Bert Bell was a visionary, but you might not be able to tell judging by his days as an Eagles owner. First, like a lawyer who makes the mistake of representing himself, he decided he could coach his team in addition to his other duties, and he took over for Wray as coach of the 1936 Eagles. Though the decision was one of necessity, saving the cost of paying a coach, it was also done in part because the franchise had a losing record in its first three seasons and appeared to regress in 1935. Bell figured he could do no worse than Wray had. After all, he had a bona fide coaching background.

He was wrong. The 1936 Eagles were the laughingstock of the NFL. On Opening Day, the Eagles upset the Giants 10–7 before more than 20,000 fans at Municipal Stadium, the team's new home after leaving the Baker Bowl. Those 20,000 fans should have savored that win, for it would be the only one that season for the Philadelphia franchise. The Eagles lost their next 11 games, including six shutouts, four of them coming in a row. Through those 11 games the team scored only 41 total points, an average of 3.7 per game. Center Henry Reese was the leading scorer on the team, with two field goals and three extra points.

This wasn't what Bell had hoped for. His plans went awry when one of the innovations he had brought to the NFL backfired on him. It was Bell's idea to hold a draft for college players, giving the weaker teams a chance to improve by allowing them the first pick of new talent. Before 1936 players were just signed by any team who could afford them.

The first NFL draft took place on February 8, 1936, at the Ritz-Carlton Hotel—a hotel owned by the Bell family—in Philadelphia. As is done today, the teams with the worst records dictated the order of the draft. So

*Jay Berwanger, winner of the first Heisman Trophy, became the first player drafted by the Eagles in the inaugural NFL Draft in 1936. Unfortunately for the franchise, he never played a down and chose instead to make his living away from the football field.* Photo courtesy of AP/Wide World Photos.

because the Eagles had the worst record of 1935, they picked first. There were nine rounds in the draft that year, with 81 players selected.

The Eagles picked the player they and the Downtown Athletic Club of New York City believed had been the best player in college football the previous year—University of Chicago quarterback Jay Berwanger, winner of the first Heisman Trophy. (It should be noted that the award was not actually called the Heisman in its first year—it was just the Most Valuable Player award for the best college football player east of the Mississippi. It was renamed the John W. Heisman Memorial Trophy, after the club's athletic director, the following year.) The Eagles had selected a young superstar. He won the *Chicago Tribune*'s Silver Football Award in 1935 as the Most Valuable Player in the Big Ten. His legendary coach, Clark Shaughnessy, called Berwanger "every football coach's dream player. You can say anything superlative about him, and I'll double it."

But there was only one problem—Berwanger didn't want to play pro football. When Philadelphia traded his rights to Chicago Bears coach George Halas, Berwanger asked for an astounding amount of money— $25,000 over two years. When Halas said no, Berwanger became a foam rubber salesman. He also wrote a sports column for the *Chicago Daily News*, refereed college football games, and, from 1936 to 1939, coached football at the University of Chicago. Berwanger even had a bit part, playing himself, in the 1936 football movie *The Big Game.* In 1954 he was inducted into the College Football Hall of Fame, and in 1989 he was included on *Sports Illustrated*'s 25-year anniversary All-America team, which honored players whose accomplishments extended beyond the football field. Despite these honors he will go down in Philadelphia sports history as the first player ever drafted by the Eagles never to play a down. They could have used him.

Bell did make a trade to help his team recover from the miserable 1936 season. He dealt end Ed Manske and the draft rights to Nebraska running back Sam Francis to the Bears for end Bill Hewitt, one of the best defensive ends in the league and a future Hall of Famer who would go on to become the franchise's first All-Pro selection at the end of the season. But the trade failed to provide much improvement on the field, as the Eagles

# TRIVIA

**What was the Eagles' record in their first decade?**

*Answers to the trivia questions are on pages 160–161.*

DID YOU KNOW . . . That on October 22, 1939, at Brooklyn's Ebbets Field, the Eagles played in the first televised pro football game, losing 23–14 to the Dodgers? The game was shown by NBC with Allan "Skip" Walz calling the action, which was broadcast in Brooklyn to an estimated 1,000 television sets.

managed just one more win in 1937, posting a 2–8–1 record. However several players had emerged to give Philadelphia fans hope—among them running back Emmett Mortell, who led the team with 312 yards rushing, and quarterback Dave Smukler, who threw for 432 yards and six touchdowns.

One of the team's only two victories, a 14–0 win, came against the Redskins, who had moved from Boston to Washington, D.C. It was the Eagles' first win in 17 games, and it was a shocker, considering that the Redskins, led by rookie quarterback Sammy Baugh, would go on to win the NFL championship that season.

The franchise seemed to be digging its way out of the abyss in 1938, when its record improved to 5–6, putting the Eagles in fourth in the Eastern Division. Then Bell the general manager made a few more moves that helped Bell the coach, acquiring two strong tackles, Drew Ellis and Ray Keeling, to bolster the offensive line.

Philadelphia lost its home opener 26–23 before 20,000 fans in a hard-fought battle against the defending champion Redskins, then beat Pittsburgh 27–7 in a game played in Buffalo before coming home to beat the Giants 14–10 before another home crowd of 20,000. The Eagles finished the season with two wins in a row, a 14–7 victory over Pittsburgh and a 21–7 win over the Lions in Detroit. Joe Carter finished third in the league in scoring with 48 points and was named to the league's All-Star second team, along with Hewitt. Smukler returned one kickoff that season for 101 yards.

Again, there was reason for hope going into the 1939 season, and Eagles fans were particularly excited about the team's number-one pick, 5'7", 150-pound quarterback Davey O'Brien, who had succeeded Sammy Baugh at Texas Christian University. In 1938 O'Brien led TCU to its first undefeated season, including a 15–7 win over Carnegie Tech in the Sugar Bowl and the national championship. He was named to 13 All-America teams and became the only college football player to win the Heisman

Trophy, the Maxwell Award, and the Walter Camp Trophy all in the same year. He signed a $10,000 contract with the Eagles and didn't disappoint, passing for 1,324 yards and being named first-team quarterback on the league's All-Star team.

But there was a dark cloud over the Eagles franchise that season, one positioned there by Bert Bell. Philadelphia's 1939 season opener was scheduled at home in Municipal Stadium against Pittsburgh. It was the same day of a doubleheader between the Philadelphia Athletics and the Boston Red Sox at Shibe Park, with an Old Timers' Game to be played in between the baseball games.

*Eagles owner Bert Bell (right) presented Texas Christian University quarterback Davey O'Brien with the Maxwell Trophy in 1939, then made him the team's number-one pick in that year's draft.* Photo courtesy of AP/Wide World Photos.

## First Picks

### The First NFL Draft

Philadelphia Eagles: Jay Berwanger, quarterback, University of Chicago

Boston Redskins: Riley Smith, end, Alabama

Brooklyn Dodgers: Dick Crayne, running back, Iowa

Chicago Bears: Joe Stydahar, tackle, West Virginia

Chicago Cardinals: Jim Lawrence, back, Texas Christian University

Detroit Lions: Sid Wagner, guard, Michigan State

Green Bay Packers: Russ Letlow, guard, San Francisco

New York Giants: Art Lewis, tackle, Ohio University

Pittsburgh Pirates: Bill Shakespeare, back, Notre Dame

Nearly 24,000 people went to Shibe Park to see the baseball games, and that kind of crowd could put a serious dent in the Eagles' attendance. So, though it was not raining, Bell postponed the scheduled opener because of "threatening" weather. An account in the Philadelphia *Evening Bulletin* questioned Bell's decision, joking that "a dark cloud passed over the sky somewhere north of Manayunk."

Bell tried to use the weather to hold off box-office losses again three weeks later, when the team was to face Brooklyn. This time it *was* raining, but as any real fan knows, that doesn't generally stop a football game. Brooklyn owner Dan Topping vehemently opposed calling off the game, and so it was played at Municipal Stadium before a crowd of only 1,880. Bell reportedly lost nearly $12,000 that day. The incident created bad blood between Bell and Topping, which the *Bulletin* called "one of the strongest feuds that the league has ever known." There were reports that Bell threatened his players with suspension and fines if they didn't beat the Dodgers in the second game the two teams played that year. It didn't work; the Eagles lost 23–14 in Brooklyn.

Nothing was working for Bell in 1941. Although the team was playing in its new stadium, Shibe Park, and despite a quarterback who was one of the best in the league, the Eagles fell back to being one of the division's worst teams, with a 2–8–1 record.

The following season was more of the same, with a 2–9 mark. O'Brien had another standout year, however, connecting with rookie end Don Looney for 58 completions. Looney led the league in catches, and O'Brien finished second in passing, completing 124 of 277 passes for 1,290 yards and five touchdowns. Despite this splendid showing, O'Brien quit football after the season ended to become an FBI agent.

After two seasons with a combined 4–17–1 mark and mounting financial losses, something had to change. Something did.

# Trading Teams

Bert Bell wasn't the only NFL owner having problems at the end of the 1940 season. The league as a whole was still going through growing pains, coming out of the Depression and on the verge of World War II.

In fact Bell wasn't even the only NFL owner in the state of Pennsylvania having problems. Pittsburgh owner Art Rooney had his own woes on the field and at the box office. He had been losing money, and not even changing the name of the team from the Pirates to the Steelers—in an effort to give it its own identity separate from that of the baseball team—seemed to help.

Rooney, like Bell, was looking for a change, and he found it in the form of millionaire businessman Alexis Thompson, a 28-year-old sports enthusiast who had inherited his family's steel fortune—$6 million at the age of 16. Thompson went on to attend Yale University and then rose to become the vice president of a prominent pharmaceutical company. He wanted to own a football team; according to the lore surrounding his tale, a New York sportswriter put Thompson and Rooney together for an October 20 meeting in New York after the Giants defeated the Steelers 12–0. But those initial talks failed to result in any deal, in large part because Thompson wanted to move the franchise to Boston. (The Redskins were no longer there, having moved to Washington, D.C., in 1936.) Boston was closer to Thompson's New York home than Pittsburgh was, but Rooney was not about to take away his hometown's football team, so he refused to sell the club. Thompson tried to convince Rooney again, traveling to Green Bay the next weekend for another meeting following the Packers' 24–3 route of the Steelers, and again Rooney turned him down.

Rooney seemed to put the notion of selling the franchise behind him; following the Steelers' 7–3 win over the Eagles on November 10, he announced that he was not going to sell the team and would retain Walt Kiesling as the coach. But if Rooney didn't want to sell his team to Thompson, there was another NFL owner who *was* interested in talking to the businessman suitor—Bell. In December there were clandestine meetings taking place between Bell, Thompson, Rooney, Kiesling, Heinie Miller (Bell's assistant coach), and the man Bell hired to take over as coach for the 1941 squad, Earle "Greasy" Neale.

On December 9—one day after the Chicago Bears made history with their 73–0 romp over the Redskins in the 1940 NFL championship game—Rooney, Bell, and Thompson announced one of the most bizarre sports deals ever made. Rooney sold the Pittsburgh Steelers to Thompson for $160,000, then turned around and bought a half interest in the Eagles, becoming partners with Bell. The two teams swapped a number of players to fit the needs of the new Bell-Rooney franchise as best they could.

Thompson said he would keep the Steelers team in Pittsburgh for at least a year, but Bell and Rooney knew Thompson wanted to move the team to Boston as soon as possible, so the two owners hatched a plan to step in by changing the name of the Eagles to the Pennsylvania Keystoners and splitting home games between Pittsburgh and Philadelphia. They even tried to plan to play all of their games—both home and away—in either Philadelphia or Pittsburgh, effectively playing an entire home schedule split between just two cities.

But Thompson didn't want to wait a year—he was looking to get out of Pittsburgh right away. He announced he was changing the name of the team to the Pittsburgh Iron Men, then proceeded to turn the operation into what was for all intents and purposes a dormant organization—he never even opened a business office in Pittsburgh. Rooney offered a suggestion that would let Thompson get out and bring Rooney back to Pittsburgh full time. "I asked him how he'd like to make a switch and let me stay in Pittsburgh and take over the Philadelphia territory himself," Rooney told writers years later, recounting the events. "That suited him because Philadelphia is so much closer to his New York headquarters, and that's how it was worked out."

# TRIVIA

**What is the name of Eagles receiver Don Looney's son, who also played in the NFL?**

*Answers to the trivia questions are on pages 160–161.*

On April 8, 1941, Rooney was back as owner of the Steelers—and it all happened before a ball had been snapped since the last time he owned the franchise. "I know we've gone around in circles, but I guess we're settled now," Rooney declared. Bell was pleased because his financial burden had been lifted, though he was now the co-owner of the Steelers rather than his hometown Philadelphia franchise.

Eleven Steelers stayed in Pittsburgh, joined by 14 former Eagles; seven Eagles stayed in Philadelphia, and 16 former Steelers joined them. Several Eagles were so unhappy with being sent to Pittsburgh that they sued Bell, and the NFL ultimately returned them to Philadelphia so they wouldn't leave the league.

All of these changes didn't seem to help much on the field, though there certainly was some early buzz for the new Eagles. The largest crowd at the time in Philadelphia pro football history showed up for the first game of the 1941 season, but those 40,000 fans went home disappointed after watching the Giants shut out the Eagles 24–0.

The disappointments continued. The Eagles went 2–8–1 under new coach Greasy Neale and his T formation style of play. Ironically, one of those wins was a 10–7 victory over the Rooney-Bell Steelers in Pittsburgh before nearly 13,000 fans. In their other matchup that season the teams tied 7–7 before more than 15,000 Philadelphia fans. But the Eagles had an exciting new quarterback named Tommy Thompson, who completed 86 of 162 passes in 1941, gaining 974 yards and eight touchdowns. Despite being blind in one eye, he was a tremendous athlete who was well-suited to the T formation and would become a top NFL quarterback.

Bell began coaching the Steelers, but after a 17–14 loss to the Cleveland Rams and the 10–7 loss to the Eagles, he stepped down and was replaced by local legend Aldo "Buff" Donelli from nearby Duquesne University. But the new coach, concerned about the uncertain nature of the NFL and the turmoil the Pittsburgh franchise had been through—and aware that coaching the college game was a better, higher profile job—tried to do both at the same time. He maintained this balancing act for five games, but when Duquesne had to play St. Mary's College in California on the road, he abandoned the Steelers, who were facing the Eagles that week. Alan Robinson, in an article for the Associated Press, wrote, "NFL commissioner Elmer

*Steelers owner Art Rooney (right), pictured with son Dan in 1966, teamed up with Eagles owner Bert Bell in 1940 to form one of the most unique—however short-lived—partnerships in league history.*
Photo courtesy of
AP/Wide World Photos.

**IF ONLY . . .** Eagles owner Bert Bell hadn't traded the draft rights to George McAfee to the Chicago Bears, the franchise might have found success much more quickly in the 1940s. Bell brought the idea of a player draft to the NFL in 1936, but he fell woefully short in benefiting from his own concept. The franchise was unable to sign any of the players it drafted in that first season, and by the time 1940 rolled around, Bell, whose team's poor finishes gave him high draft choices, began selling those players off, trading the rights to George McAfee to the Chicago Bears along with the team's top place in the 1941 draft.

Layden, one of Notre Dame's famed Four Horsemen, was so angry he banished Donelli from the league. The Steelers then rehired former coach Walt Kiesling as the third and final coach of a 1–9–1 season. Donelli didn't return until three years later as the Cleveland Rams' coach."

In Philadelphia, despite the losing season, Thompson was excited about finally owning an NFL franchise and much happier to be in the city of brotherly love, rather than the steel city. He told reporters he was "extremely happy to come to Philadelphia. I tried to get the Philadelphia franchise before I purchased the Pittsburgh club. I know Philadelphia is a great sports town and appreciates a good team. We'll give them that kind of club no matter how much money or effort it takes."

Thompson tried to make a change to his team's uniforms, coming up with an innovative jersey-numbering system. The first number on a player's jersey indicated his offensive position. For quarterbacks, it was 1; right halfbacks, 2; fullbacks, 3; tailbacks, 4; centers, 5; guards, 6; tackles, 7; and ends, 8. The second number identified the individual player, at a time when players' names were not on the backs of uniforms. But the other owners would not go along with Thompson's plan, so the idea died until 32 years later, when the NFL finally instituted a jersey-numbering system of its own.

The Eagles didn't have much to show for the 1942 season, winning only two games while losing nine. And again, one of those victories, the 24–14 season opener, came against their old owner Bell in Pittsburgh.

But the stunner came after losing to the Giants 14–0 at home on November 8, when Neale reportedly suffered a heart attack during the game, yet stayed on the bench and continued to coach through the rest of the game (and the season). If he did indeed have a heart attack—an improbable diagnosis—maybe it was because he had a premonition of what was to come in 1943.

If the Eagles-Steelers franchise swap had been bizarre, what was coming would trump it.

# A Football Innovator: Greasy Neale

Alfred Earle Neale was born November 5, 1891, in Parkersburg, West Virginia. A few years after that, "Greasy" Neale was born on the streets of Parkersburg while playing with some boyhood friends. The story goes that Neale nicknamed one of his friends "Dirty," so the friend came back and called Neale "Greasy." The name stuck, luckily, because someone as talented and destined for stardom as Earle Neale would certainly need a memorable nickname to match the acclaim that he would receive as one of the most successful coaches in Philadelphia Eagles history, leading his teams to three straight Eastern Division titles and consecutive NFL championships in 1948 and 1949.

As an end at West Virginia Wesleyan, Neale caught 14 straight passes when the school upset the University of West Virginia 19–14 in 1912, the school's first-ever win over that rival. Neale was a talented basketball player as well, and he once reached the semifinals of the West Virginia Amateur Golf Tournament. He graduated in 1914 and played for the Canton Bulldogs in the pre-NFL days, then went to Muskingum College as football coach in 1915. Neale returned to West Virginia Wesleyan to coach in 1916 and 1917. After military service in World War I he played football for the Dayton Triangles, a football team predating the NFL, in 1918. He also coached at Marietta College in 1919 and 1920 and at Washington and Jefferson in 1921 and 1922, leading his team to the Rose Bowl in that 1922 season. He coached at the University of Virginia from 1923 through 1928 and at West Virginia University from 1931 through 1933. His overall college record was 78–55–11.

Neale was also a standout baseball player while growing up and at West Virginia Wesleyan, and he played eight seasons in the Major Leagues for the Cincinnati Reds, then the Philadelphia Phillies from

1916 to 1924. He played for the Reds team that beat the Chicago White Sox in the infamous 1919 World Series, the year of the Black Sox scandal, when eight Chicago players were banned from baseball for life for allegedly conspiring with gamblers to throw the Series. Neale hit .357 for the Reds in that Series.

Torn between baseball and football, Neale's Major League accomplishments were all achieved while he held down a variety of college football coaching jobs. In an article he wrote for *Collier's* magazine in 1951, Neale said that baseball was his passion. "My first love was baseball, and my consuming ambition was to become a big leaguer," Neale wrote. "The football I played as a youngster was merely a fill-in to keep busy until it was warm enough to play baseball."

Despite those feelings, football was Neale's calling. When he joined heralded Yale University as an assistant coach in charge of the offense in

*Former Eagles coach Greasy Neale (fourth from left) is pictured during his induction into the College Football Hall of Fame in 1967.* Photo courtesy of Bettmann/CORBIS.

That the NFL used to be full of great nicknames? Back in the early days of the league, men had nicknames that they could be proud of—names that belonged on a football field, such as "Greasy" Neale, John "Blood" McNally, Clyde "Bulldog" Turner, and, of course, the legendary Earl "Curly" Lambeau.

1934, he caught the attention of the New York and Boston metropolitan area media, and his reputation as a strong offensive coach grew.

Despite his high-profile new position at Yale, Neale was still Greasy from Parkersburg, as he made quite clear when he first arrived. School officials there urged reporters not to use the nickname Greasy. But Neale told the writers, "Yale or no Yale, you fellows want to call me Greasy, go ahead."

Alexis Thompson took notice of Neale, and, when he bought the Eagles in 1941, he hired Neale as coach. The story goes that after Neale was hired, he spent long periods of time studying game film of the 1940 NFL championship game in which the Chicago Bears trampled the Washington Redskins 73–0. This was the game with which the Bears changed the game of football by refining the T formation to create an offensive juggernaut. Offensive guru Clark Shaughnessy, the former head coach at the University of Chicago, taught the Bears the technique. He had come to be known as the master of the T formation, in which there are three running backs in the backfield, and the center, quarterback, and running backs line up in the shape of a *T*. But if Shaughnessy was the master of the T formation, Neale would become the grand master, imitating and then improving the Bears' T formation strategy.

Additionally, along with Thompson and Eagles general manager Harry Thayer, Neale developed an elaborate method for compiling complete information on all college football players. Years later Neale recalled the skepticism their system initially received: "We had 68 books that we took into the second draft meeting we attended. No team had ever done this before. They laughed at us, but you can bet they stopped after we got ourselves men like [Steve] Van Buren with that system."

It took a while for Neale's coaching and personnel philosophies to show results—his teams were 2–8–1 in 1941 and 2–9 in 1942. But two years later the Eagles were a winning team, eventually becoming the team of the decade. From 1944—the year they drafted Van Buren, who would go on to be a Hall of Fame back—through 1949, Neale's Eagles finished second three times and in first place three times. The Eagles won the NFL championship in 1948 and again in 1949. It was the only team to win back-to-back titles by shutting out their opponents: the Chicago Cardinals 7–0 in 1948 and the Los Angeles Rams 14–0 in 1949. The win in 1949 was by a team that included a talented young linebacker named Chuck Bednarik. Neale would be named NFL Coach of the Year in 1948 and 1949.

Neale's offense was led by the passing of quarterback Tommy Thompson, the pass catching of future Hall of Fame end Pete Pihos, and Van Buren. Defensively, Neale developed the so-called "Eagle Defense," which would be a mainstay around the league for years to come. Their defensive strategy eventually spawned another NFL favorite, the 4-3 defense, which is still used today.

It wasn't all formations and talent, though. Neale was a colorful character and made no bones about relying on superstitions for help as well. In his *Collier's* article he wrote, "I'm terribly superstitious and wear the same suit and the same hat to each game if we are winning. I even drive out to the park by the same route."

If Neale believed in omens, he received a bad one in 1949 when the Eagles were sold to a group led by businessman Jim Clark. The new owner clashed with Neale during the 1950 season and, after the Eagles fell to a 6–6 record, including an embarrassing 35–10 opening-game loss to the Cleveland Browns before a home crowd of more than 71,000 fans, Neale was fired—by telegram. He was vacationing at Lake Worth, Florida, in February 1951 when he got a telegram from Clark that said: "You will be paid for the one year remaining on your contract, but you are no longer the coach of the Philadelphia Eagles."

**DID YOU KNOW . . .** That Greasy Neale is the only man to have played in a World Series (with the Cincinnati Reds in 1919), coached a football team in the Rose Bowl (Washington and Jefferson, 1922), and won an NFL title (two in 10 years with the Eagles)? He was traded from the Reds to the Phillies, along with pitcher Jimmy Ring, in 1920 for future Hall of Fame pitcher Eppa Rixey.

It was a shock from which Neale never fully recovered. "It was a complete surprise," he said years later. "Clark told me that I could coach the Eagles as long as he had the club. It liked to kill my wife. She died two months later."

Neale finished his 10-year career as the Eagles coach with a 66–44–5 record (including postseason) and two NFL championships. He was inducted into the College Football Hall of Fame in 1967 and the Pro Football Hall of Fame in 1969. Four years later Neale passed away at the age of 71. Until Andy Reid surpassed him in 2004, Neale remained the winningest coach in Philadelphia Eagles history. He will always be known as the coach who changed the franchise from losers to winners for the first time, and gave Eagles fans their first taste of a rare achievement for the organization—an NFL championship.

# The Steagles Take the Stage

World War II presented many problems for the NFL, both on and off the field. With so many men serving in the military, just getting enough players in uniform—a football uniform, that is—was a struggle. By the time the 1943 season started, 376 players who had appeared on NFL rosters during the previous three years were serving in the military. Two would be killed in action—Brooklyn's Don Wemple and Washington's Keith Birlem. The box office also suffered; the nation's attention was directed toward the war effort, and no one was particularly excited about a watered-down version of a sport that was still struggling just to find its place in the American sports and entertainment landscape.

League officials met on April 1, 1943, and made some significant decisions. The Cleveland Rams were allowed to disband for the duration of the war because the team's owners, Fred Levy and Dan Reeves, were in the service. They would, however, maintain control of their players and draft picks until the team was reactivated. In the meantime, the players were lent to other teams. As it turned out, the Rams were out of the action for only one year, returning in 1944 and winning the championship in 1945.

Substitutions had been restricted, but now free substitution was allowed, though not completely accepted by all. The league adopted the revolutionary rule largely as a hedge against the manpower shortage. With so many regular players absent, teams had to get by with many players of more limited abilities. In addition, active rosters were cut back from 33 to 28 players per game, helmets became mandatory, and a 10-game schedule (one game fewer than the previous year) was adopted.

The notion of having one Pennsylvania team—a combined Eagles and Steelers squad—resurfaced in 1943. "Don't you think [two teams]'d

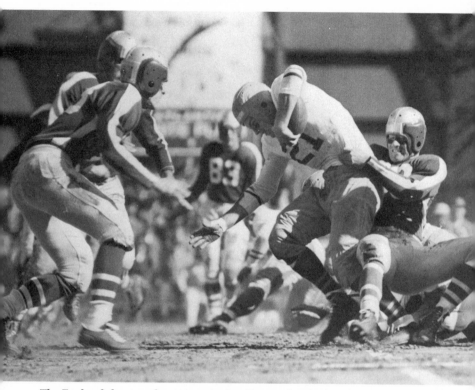

*The Eagles defense makes a stop against Boston during the 1944 season, in which the team went 7–1–1 for its best record to date.* Photo courtesy of Bettmann/CORBIS.

be able to come up with enough good players for one team?" Bert Bell wondered. Both teams' problems were accentuated by the fact that they were so bad on the field, and given the paucity of available talent, there was little hope of improvement anytime soon.

"Good prospects were draft material, all right, but not for the NFL," *Philadelphia Inquirer* reporter Tom Infield wrote. So the Eagles and the Steelers ceased to exist in 1943, coming together to form the Philadelphia-Pittsburgh Eagles-Steelers—known to most as the Steagles. The Eagles had 20 players on the roster, while the Steelers had 11. The best players from both teams were retained to form the Steagles.

Greasy Neale and Walt Kiesling, who were rivals before the merger, ran the 28-man team together, but the two didn't get along. Kiesling wanted to run the traditional single-wing formation, while Neale had begun using a T formation in Philadelphia. Their disagreements got so bad that Kiesling and Neale walked off the field after a heated argument in practice the Friday before one game. They returned for the game, but the players were nonetheless stunned. "Each one wanted to be the head honcho," defensive back Ernie Steele said. "They were like two little kids. They both quit. They walked into the locker room."

Despite the coaching differences, the experiment proved to be successful on the field, as the Steagles posted a winning record in 1943, going 5–4–1, playing four home games at Shibe Park in Philadelphia and two games at Forbes Field in Pittsburgh. They drew more than 34,000 fans in Pittsburgh for the final game of the season, a 38–28 loss to the Green Bay Packers. Their largest crowd in Philadelphia, nearly 29,000 fans, saw a 14–14 tie against the hated Washington Redskins. It was the first winning season in Eagles history and only the second for Pittsburgh.

The average attendance at NFL games jumped by a third in 1943, up to 24,228 per game. That was a new per-game record (and the best until after the war in 1945), but the total attendance of 969,128 for 40 games was down from the million-plus years of 1939–41, when the league played 55 games a season.

Eagles owner Thompson decided he wanted his team to be separate again and to play all home games in Philadelphia, so the Steagles were done away with after 1943. Rooney, owner of the Steelers, was still looking to create a partnership to share his financial burdens, and he soon formed another merger, this one with the Chicago Cardinals. That move was not as successful as the Steagles, however, as the combined team—called the "Card-Pitts" by some fans—lost every game that season.

The 1944 season saw the greatest success of any Eagles team to date. They went 7–1–2, good for second place in the Eastern Conference, including an impressive 24–17 win over the New York Giants on the road, in a contest that drew 42,639. The team's largest draw at home was 34,035, a crowd that watched the Eagles lose to the Bears 28–7. But that was the team's only loss, and it finished the season with two home victories over the Brooklyn Tigers (formerly known as the Dodgers) and the Cleveland Rams. The

# TRIVIA

**Who played five seasons at quarterback for the Eagles before becoming a very successful NFL head coach?**

*Answers to the trivia questions are on pages 160–161.*

**DID YOU KNOW . . .** That Steve Van Buren, one of the greatest running backs in the history of the Eagles franchise and a Hall of Fame player, set a number of records with Philadelphia in the 1940s, including one that still stands today: most touchdowns in one season (18 in 1945)? Van Buren scored 15 of them rushing, two of them on touchdown catches, and one on a kick return.

Eagles were led by rookie running back Steve Van Buren, who rushed for 444 yards (fifth best in the league) on 80 carries, returned 15 punts for a 15.3 average and one touchdown, and had eight kickoffs for a 33.3 average and another touchdown. He was the runner-up for NFL Rookie of the Year and was also named to the All-Pro team.

Before the 1945 season began, the Eagles played an historic exhibition game for *The Philadelphia Inquirer* Charities organization. In front of the largest crowd ever to watch a pro football game at that time—an estimated 90,000 people—the Eagles beat the Green Bay Packers 28–21. They then won their opener at Shibe Park, a 21–6 victory over the Chicago Cardinals before a crowd of 25,581. But they lost their next two, on the road, to Detroit and Washington. Philadelphia finished strong, though, winning six of their final seven games, including the season finale, a 35–7 victory over the Boston Yanks. With Van Buren—who led the league with 832 yards on 143 carries and 15 touchdowns—the Eagles finished with a 7–3 record for their second straight second-place finish in the Eastern Division.

There was much hope and optimism in the country following World War II, as well as opportunity for new ventures. The NFL saw the return of many players who had been serving in the armed forces, but the league also saw the rise of a competitor—a new organization called the All-American Football Conference (AAFC), with teams in New York, Brooklyn, Buffalo, Cleveland, Chicago, San Francisco, Miami (later Baltimore), and Los Angeles. Fortunately for the Eagles, the AAFC had no franchise in Philadelphia. The new league raided NFL teams for 30 players; they tried to recruit the Eagles' Roy Zimmerman, Jack Ferrante, and Van Buren, but were unsuccessful. The NFL made a move to strengthen itself by electing a new commissioner to steer the league through these competitive times—a familiar name, former Eagles owner Bert Bell.

Philadelphia fell to 6–5 in 1946, but that was still good for second place in the Eastern Division. After four straight winning seasons under Neale, it appeared as if the Eagles were building a winning organization. By the time the 1947 season started the Eagles were considered contenders for the league title. They were helped that year by the arrival of future Hall of Fame end Pete Pihos, who had been drafted by the team in 1945 but served two years of military service before being able to join the club. Neale's team finished first in the Eastern Conference with an 8–4 record, tying with the franchise they had been linked to for the entire decade—who else but the Steelers—and setting up a playoff game in Pittsburgh between the two. The Eagles triumphed 21–0, led by quarterback Thompson's touchdown passes to Van Buren and Ferrante.

The Eagles would now face the Chicago Cardinals in the NFL championship game at Comiskey Park. On a brutally cold December afternoon Philadelphia was defeated 28–21. The Cardinals scored on a 44-yard run, a 75-yard punt return by Charlie Trippi, and two 70-yard runs by Elmer Angsman, who had 10 carries worth 159 yards that day. The Eagles came back with a 53-yard Thompson–to–Pat McHugh pass, but fell short of winning the championship. Still, they had taken yet another step toward winning that league crown.

# "Wham Bam" Van Buren Takes the Eagles to the Top

Football is, for all intents and purposes, a game of power. If the other team can't stop you, your team generally wins the game. Stripped away of all the formations, patterns, and strategies, the essence of the game comes down to power.

And if all that is true, then Steve Van Buren was football in its purest form. He was one of the most powerful runners ever to wear an NFL uniform and perhaps the greatest running back in Philadelphia Eagles history, leading the Eagles to two NFL championships. He is right there among the great power runners of the game, along with players like Marion Motley, Jim Brown, Larry Csonka, and Jerome Bettis.

Was he as good as even the great Jim Thorpe? At least one of his former Eagles coaches believed so. "Thorpe was a bigger man than Van Buren, outweighed him by 10 pounds and was two inches taller," Philadelphia line coach John Kellison told *The Sporting News* in a 1948 interview. "Yet Steve does the same things as Thorpe. There is one difference. When Thorpe hit, he did so with his knees. Steve uses his shoulder—and with terrific power."

As a youngster Van Buren was an unlikely force of nature. Born December 28, 1920, in La Cerba, Honduras, he was orphaned when he was very young and sent to New Orleans to live with his grandparents. He failed to make the Warren Easton High School football team as a 125-pound high school sophomore, but as a senior he played well enough to win a scholarship to Louisiana State University. But even at LSU he spent most of his time as the blocking back for their star runner, a future Major League baseball player and manager by the name of Alvin Dark. But Neale and the Eagles' brain trust, who had developed a sophisticated method of scouting and evaluating talent that was ahead of its time, selected Van Buren as their number one pick in 1944.

It was an inspired selection. The 6'1', 210-pound Van Buren had a huge impact on the Eagles' offense as soon as he arrived. Philadelphia was 7–1–2 in 1944 with Van Buren rushing for 444 yards (an average of 5.6 yards per carry), running back kickoffs (for an average of 33.3 yards per return), and bringing back punts (at a clip of 15.3 yards per punt return). In Van Buren's second season the Eagles posted a 7–3 record while the big back led the league in rushing (with 832 yards for a remarkable 5.8-yard-per-carry average), kickoff returns (averaging 29 yards per return), and scoring (crossing the goal line for a career-high 18 touchdowns).

*Steve Van Buren, pictured during a tribute in Philadelphia, was arguably the best running back the Eagles have ever had and the cornerstone for two championships.*

DID YOU KNOW . . . That there have been rumors that Eagles coach Greasy Neale really wanted to sign Steve Van Buren's running mate at LSU, Alvin Dark? Dark instead pursued a successful career in Major League baseball as a player and manager. He played 14 seasons, primarily with the New York Giants, and had 2,089 career hits, 1,064 runs scored, and a .289 career average. He also managed for 13 years with the San Francisco Giants, the Kansas City Athletics, the Cleveland Indians, the Oakland Athletics, and the San Diego Padres, compiling a record of 994–954.

Philadelphia had never finished better than fourth place until Van Buren came on the scene in 1944. That year they finished second; they did the same during two other seasons with Van Buren. They also won three straight divisional titles and took the NFL title in 1948 and 1949. Van Buren rushed for over 1,000 yards in two 12-game seasons—1,008 in 1947 and a career-high 1,146 in the 1949 championship season.

Van Buren was an All-NFL selection in each of his first six seasons, and by the time he was done playing, after the 1951 season, he had rushed for 5,860 career yards, averaging 4.4 yards per carry, and caught 45 passes for 523 yards. The big back also gained a reputation as a punishing runner who would come to be known by a variety of nicknames—"Wham Bam" and "Blockbuster" among them.

Van Buren saved his best performances for the biggest games. In the Eagles' 7–0 win over the Chicago Cardinals in the 1948 title game, Van Buren scored the game's only touchdown and ran for 98 yards. One year later, in the 1949 championship game, Van Buren carried the ball 31 times for 196 yards in Philadelphia's 14–0 victory over the Los Angeles Rams on a muddy field.

"I wanted to get tackled in that game," Van Buren told the *Philadelphia Daily News* years later in an interview. "I'd run into guys just to get tackled. I was exhausted."

## TRIVIA

**How many consecutive 100-yard games did Steven Van Buren have in 1947?**

*Answers to the trivia questions are on pages 160–161.*

"He was out of this world that day," receiver Jack Ferrante told the *Daily News*. "He just ran like every breath was his last. God bless him, he was one heckuva football player."

The banging and bruising would eventually break down his body, but as he told the *Daily News*, Van Buren did all he could to stay on the football field for as many years as he could:

> I used to take maybe six shots [painkilling injections] each half. Into the ribs. And the big toe. Once you hurt that big toe, it never gets better. So I used to get shots with a needle that long under the bottom of the toe. The only time it bothered me was when they hit the bone. The needle would bend and sometimes it would break. I didn't like it. When they hit the bone, it really hurt .... And anybody would give it to you. Everybody wanted to shoot me with the needle.
>
> If I could have run long, I could have been better. If I could have run long ....

Elected to the Pro Football Hall of Fame in 1965, Van Buren said he didn't play for the glory. He played because he loved football. His love helped bring the Philadelphia Eagles into their championship era.

# Titletown I

The high hopes fans had for Greasy Neale's Philadelphia Eagles going into the 1948 season fell like a thud in an early game in Chicago; the Eagles once again lost to the Cardinals by seven points in a rematch of the 1947 title game, this time going down 21–14. The league, though, suffered a far greater loss that day when one of the Cardinals, tackle Stan Mauldin, had a heart attack after the game and died. (Later in the season when Philadelphia had clinched the division title while the Cardinals were in a battle for their division with the Bears, the Eagles players voted that Mauldin's widow should receive a full share of Philadelphia's championship game money regardless of the outcome of the Cards' season.)

The Eagles left for Los Angeles to face the Rams in their next contest. When they blew a 28–0 lead, allowing the Rams to tie the score, Philadelphia fans back home must have wondered if their preseason optimism had been misplaced.

Maybe all the players needed was some home cooking.

Back home at Shibe Park, the team that nearly 23,000 Eagles fans saw in the first home game of the season was not the same losing squad from the first two games. They destroyed the New York Giants 45–0, the second worst defeat in the history of the Giants franchise. Quarterback Tommy Thompson threw touchdown passes to Pete Pihos and Ernie Steele and ran for another touchdown, while Steve Van Buren also ran one in.

Just in case Philadelphia fans thought that win was a fluke, the Eagles turned in another excellent performance in the fourth game of the season, this time against the rival Washington Redskins at Griffith Stadium—another 45–0 victory before nearly 36,000 fans. It was the Redskins' worst-ever defeat in regular-season play. The Eagles' offense,

**By the NUMBERS** **45–0**—During the Eagles' 1948 championship season they defeated the New York Giants 45–0 in week three, followed by a 45–0 win over the Washington Redskins the following week. Four weeks later they beat the Boston Yanks 45–0. They did their best to repeat their achievement against Detroit in the season finale, as the offense scored 45 points again. But the defense didn't cooperate, allowing the Lions to score 21 points.

meanwhile, had 28 first downs, a new league record. Van Buren rushed for three touchdowns, and the Eagles were on their way.

Their next home game drew more than 37,000 fans for a 12–7 win over the Chicago Bears. After that they manhandled their next five opponents with a 34–7 victory at Pittsburgh against the Steelers; a 35–14 win over the Giants in New York; a third 45–0 win, this one over Boston at home; followed by another home victory, a 42–21 win over the Redskins; and finishing up with a 17–0 shutout against the Steelers.

The Eagles' juggernaut was derailed by the Boston Yanks in a 37–14 defeat; because the team had already clinched the Eastern Division, Van Buren sat out with an injury. They came back to finish the season with their favorite offensive score—45—beating the Lions 45–21 at home for the regular-season finale and finishing the season with a 9–2–1 record. The offense had one of the most impressive performances the NFL had ever seen, scoring 376 points while holding opposing teams to only 156.

Thompson led the league with 25 touchdown passes and only 11 interceptions, completing 141 of 246 passes for 1,965 yards. Van Buren rushed for 945 yards on 201 carries, scoring 10 touchdowns. Pihos pulled down 46 catches for 766 yards, a 16.7 yard-per-catch average, and 11 touchdowns, while Jack Ferrante caught 28 passes for 444 yards. Fullback Joe Muha seldom carried the ball but was a strong blocker, a tough linebacker, and the NFL's leading punter with a 47.2 yard average. Vic Sears and Al Wistert were all-league linemen, while Cliff Patton led the league's kickers with eight field goals.

Meanwhile the Chicago Cardinals had won their second straight Western Division crown with an 11–1–0 record, the best in the history of the franchise. To insure their title they had defeated their crosstown rivals, the Bears, on the final Sunday of the season. The Cardinals were led by

*Pictured from left to right: Steve Van Buren, Pete Pihos, and Bobby Thomason following the Eagles' back-to-back championships.*

their dream backfield: Charlie Trippi, Paul Christman, Pat Harder, and Elmer Angsman. They were 3½-point favorites to win against the Eagles, even with their quarterback, Christman, out with a broken finger on his throwing hand.

**TRIVIA**

**How many first-quarter points did opposing teams score against the Eagles in 1948?**

*Answers to the trivia questions are on pages 160–161.*

It was a much-anticipated game. Nearly 37,000 tickets were sold for the contest at Shibe Park. The game was to be broadcast on a 46-station radio and television network, and more than 200 writers from across the country were expected to attend. However, on the morning of the December 19 championship game, one of the worst blizzards in Philadelphia's history struck. A tarpaulin that had covered the field for a week created a problem on the morning of the game—it took nearly 100 men to pull the snow-filled cover off the field. As the snow continued to fall, the yard lines were wiped out and all yardage had to be estimated. Commissioner Bert Bell considered postponing the game, with Neale's backing. "I don't want to work all year for one big climactic game and then lose on a break like this," Neale said. But the Cardinals wanted to play, and Bell consented to let the game continue.

More than 29,000 fans braved the snow to be a part of this historic Philadelphia occasion. They saw their team nearly take the game from the first moment with a 65-yard pass from Thompson to Ferrante, but an offside call nullified the play. There would be no such big plays again, and neither team scored in the first half.

Before the end of the third quarter, Chicago's Ray Mallouf fumbled and Frank "Bucko" Kilroy recovered for the Eagles on the Cardinals' 17. The Eagles moved the ball down to the 5-yard line, where Van Buren punched it in, and Philadelphia led 7–0. The Cardinals were never able to respond under the blizzard conditions, and the Eagles won their first NFL championship with one touchdown and an extra point. Greasy Neale's salvation of the Eagles was complete.

The Philadelphia players earned $1,540 for their winning effort, while the Cardinals each got a check for $874. Four Eagles—Van Buren, Thompson, Pihos, and Al Wistert—were named to the Associated Press and United Press International All-Pro teams, and Van Buren was named the NFL's Most Valuable Player.

# Titletown II

The NFL continued to experiment and change in 1949. As in 1943, the league approved free substitution, this time for a one-year period. The Boston Yanks moved to New York and became the Bulldogs. And even though the Eagles were the defending league champions, they started the season facing change as well. Alexis Thompson put the franchise up for sale. There were a number of bidders, including entertainers Bob Hope and Frankie Laine, but the team was sold to a syndicate headed by Philadelphia businessman James P. Clark on January 15. Clark led a group of 100 investors, each of whom reportedly paid $3,000 for a share in the team. They were called the "Happy Hundred" or the "100 Brothers." The group included a number of leaders in politics and business.

The Eagles turned in an even more impressive season than they had the previous year, rolling over the league with an 11–1 record, with their only loss a 38–21 defeat at the hands of the Bears in Chicago in week four of the 1949 season after winning their first three games. Neale's outfit went on to win their next eight games, finishing with a 17–3 victory over the New York Giants before a home crowd of more than 21,000 fans. Their biggest crowd of the season—38,230, also the largest regular-season crowd in franchise history—came to watch the Eagles easily defeat the power of the Western Conference, the Los Angeles Rams, 38–14.

This Eagles offense scored 364 points, a slight drop from the year before, but the defense held opponents to a remarkable 134 points, 22 less than the 1948 defense. Tommy Thompson completed 116 of 214 passes for 1,727 yards and 16 touchdowns. Steve Van Buren rushed for 1,146 yards on 263 carries—leading the league for the fourth time—and scored 11 touchdowns, also tops in the NFL, while Bosh Pritchard rushed for 506 yards. Jack Ferrante caught 34 passes, as did Pete Pihos, with Ferrante gaining 508 yards and Pihos 484. Kicker Cliff Patton scored 69 points, going nine for 18 in field goals and hitting on 42 of 43 extra points. In their 49–14 win over the Washington Redskins, Eagles fans saw Patton set a new NFL record when he kicked seven straight extra points, running his consecutive streak to a new league record of 77 straight extra points.

The two teams' next match-up was a record setter; in Philadelphia's 44–21 win over Washington the Eagles never punted, equaling the record set in 1934 by the New York Giants. Tommy Thompson threw four touchdown passes, the longest one a 70-yarder to Clyde Scott, while the Philadelphia defense had five interceptions. Two weeks later, when the Eagles clinched the Eastern Division with a 34–17 win over the Steelers at Shibe Park, Van Buren rushed for 205 yards—only 10 yards short of the NFL record.

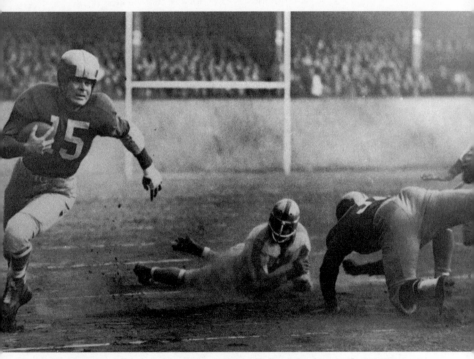

*Steve Van Buren picks up a first down against the Giants during the 1949 championship season.* Photo courtesy of Bettmann/CORBIS.

All-1940s
Team

The Eagles had a team for the ages in their first full decade, with five future Hall of Fame players on their roster.

| Position | Name |
| --- | --- |
| Coach | Greasy Neale |
| *Offense* | |
| End | Pete Pihos |
| | Jack Ferrante |
| Tackle | Al Wistert |
| | Vic Sears |
| Guard | Frank "Bucko" Kilroy |
| | Cliff Patton |
| Center | Vic Lindskog |
| Quarterback | Tommy Thompson |
| Halfback | Steve Van Buren |
| | Bosh Pritchard |
| Fullback | Jim Parmer |
| *Defense* | |
| End | John Green |
| | Pete Pihos |
| Tackle | Vic Sears |
| | Mike Jarmoluk |
| Guard | Frank "Bucko" Kilroy |
| Linebacker | Chuck Bednarik |
| | Alex Wojciechowicz |
| Back | Russ Craft |
| | Ernie Steele |
| | Roy Zimmerman |
| | Frank Reagan |

The offensive line received a boost with the additions of hard-nosed rookie center and defensive linebacker Chuck Bednarik and tackle Mike Jarmoluk, who, at 6'5" and 265 pounds, was the biggest man ever to wear an Eagles uniform up to that point.

The Eagles would bring all this size, speed, and power to Los Angeles to face the Rams—the team they had manhandled earlier that season—in the NFL championship game. There was a lot of excitement in Los Angeles—40,000 tickets had been sold, with another 30,000 fans expected to show up for the city's first major professional sports title game. However it rained continuously the night before and continued to do so throughout the game. Both teams wanted to postpone to the following Sunday—Christmas Day, December 25—but former Eagles owner and NFL commissioner Bert Bell refused to call off the game. So only 22,245 fans came to watch a methodical contest played in the rain and mud.

The Eagles took a 7–0 lead in the second quarter on a 31-yard touchdown pass from Thompson to Pihos. The weather seemed to work in the Eagles' favor in the third quarter when Rams quarterback Bob Waterfield failed to punt the muddy ball quickly enough to avoid a block by end Leo Skladany, who grabbed the ball at the Rams' 2-yard line and rolled in for the touchdown and a 14–0 Eagles lead.

Philadelphia was able to control the ball for most of the game because of the workhorse effort of Van Buren, who carried the ball 31 times for 196 yards, breaking the championship game record of 159 yards held by Elmer Angsman of the Chicago Cardinals (a record coincidentally achieved in the Cardinals' win over the Eagles in the 1947 title game). Van Buren carried the ball 75 times, gaining 320 yards and breaking a record held by Bronko Nagurski (who carried the ball 57 times for 214 yards with the Chicago Bears in four title games, one more game than Van Buren). Los Angeles only managed to gain 21 team rushing yards, breaking a Washington record by one yard (the Redskins rushed for only 22 yards during their brutal 73–0 defeat at the hands of the

**DID YOU KNOW . . .** That the Boston Yanks became the New York Bulldogs in 1949 and that the Eagles shut them out twice that same year—once by a score of 7–0 in New York's home opener and again by a score of 42–0 at home later in the season? The Eagles would not play in Massachusetts again until they traveled there to play the Patriots in 1977.

Chicago Bears in the 1940 championship game). The Eagles offense netted 342 yards, the Rams only 119.

Despite the win, the share for Eagles players was only $1,000, about $600 less than what it would have been had there been no rain to keep the crowd away.

The 14–0 win marked the second straight championship game shutout for the Eagles, something that had never been done before and has never been matched since. As Bednarik once said, looking back on that 1949 team, "I think we belong with the best teams ever. Look what we accomplished."

Sadly, what they accomplished would have to be enough for Eagles fans for quite some time to come.

# Concrete Charlie: The Incomparable Chuck Bednarik

There's a term that is used these days to describe throwback athletes—the ones who define what a particular sport is all about when it's stripped of all the frills and "bling." That term is *old school*. Nobody in all of sports was more old school than Philadelphia Eagles great Chuck Bednarik. He was as talented and tough a player as ever put on an NFL uniform, and he was synonymous with the Eagles franchise for more than a decade, anchoring two of the team's NFL championships.

Born May 1, 1925, in the steel town of Bethlehem, Pennsylvania, Charles Philip "Chuck" Bednarik led Liberty High School to an undefeated season in 1942, his junior year. Like so many men of "the Greatest Generation," Bednarik went off to fight for his country in World War II. In the Army Air Corps he flew 30 combat missions over Germany as a gunner on a B-24 in 1944 and 1945. "How we survived, I don't know," Bednarik said during a profile on ESPN Classic. "From then on, great things happened for me."

Bednarik came out of the service in 1945 and enrolled at the University of Pennsylvania, intending to become a football coach and teacher. He soon made his presence known on the football field for the Quakers. In 1948 he became the first offensive lineman to ever win the Maxwell Award (given to the nation's top football player) and also finished third in the Heisman balloting. However he was just as good at linebacker (as his NFL career would show). Eventually, the award for the best college football player in the nation would be called the Chuck Bednarik Award.

The 1947 Quakers went undefeated for the first time in 39 years, led by a defense that allowed only 35 points in their eight games. The only blemish in the 7–0–1 season was against Army, who tied them 7–7.

*Chuck Bednarik developed his reputation as football's "Sixty-Minute Man" while playing both center and linebacker, and he was called "Concrete Charlie" because a sportswriter said he was as hard as the concrete he sold in the off-season.*

The Eagles drafted the 6'2", 230-pound Bednarik with their number one pick in 1949. Although he had been a devastating two-way player in college, he came into the league as a center. But he was soon to become one of the last of the two-way players in the NFL, a standout at both center and linebacker, and would eventually earn himself quite a reputation as a "Sixty-Minute Man." The Eagles began playing him at linebacker in 1951, although not because he was a washout at center. On the contrary, Bednarik was named All-Pro in 1949 and 1950 and was the heart of the offensive line on the Eagles' championship teams in 1948 and 1949. But he was too valuable not to use at linebacker, where he would be named All-Pro six times.

Bednarik sold concrete in the off-season, earning himself the nickname "Concrete Charlie" from *Philadelphia Bulletin* sportswriter Hugh Brown, who wrote that Bednarik was "as hard as the concrete he sells."

Bednarik credited his first coach in Philadelphia, the legendary Earle "Greasy" Neale, for getting him off to a good start as a pro football player. "I admired him so much," Bednarik said. "He had the most influence on my career."

Bednarik made $12,000 as the first-round pick in 1949 and received a $3,000 bonus in addition. Said Bednarik, recalling his first contract: "I bought a brand-new house for $14,500 and a brand-new Pontiac for $2,200. The most I ever made was $27,000. The reason was simple—there was no television. ... Now players come out and hold for extra points and make a half million dollars. I don't understand the pro football players of today, who are overpaid. The amount of money pro football players make boggles my mind."

If television had had the presence back then that it does now, Bednarik would have been one of its biggest stars, particularly because of two memorable plays that would have been perennial favorites on the highlight reels. Both were devastating tackles that came during the Eagles' 1960 championship year.

In a November 20 game against the New York Giants at Yankee Stadium

## TRIVIA

**What did Chuck Bednarik say during a College Football Hall of Fame induction when asked about the legendary hit he put on New York Giants superstar (and later *Monday Night Football* fixture) Frank Gifford?**

*Answers to the trivia questions are on pages 160–161.*

**By the NUMBERS**

**8**—Chuck Bednarik was named to eight Pro Bowls, the most in Eagles history. The 60-minute man was also named the Pro-Bowl Most Valuable Player as a linebacker in 1954.

(which the Eagles would win 17–10), Bednarik hit Giants receiver Frank Gifford with a brutal blow that became the most famous tackle in NFL history, captured forever in an infamous photograph of Bednarik standing over a fallen Gifford. The star receiver with the good looks and glamorous reputation would be out of football for a year and a half thanks to the hit delivered by Bednarik. "He was doing a down-and-in pattern, and I saw him coming," Bednarik said. "I just hit him high in the chest about as hard as I could. His head snapped, and he went flying one way and the ball went flying another. It was one of the hardest tackles I ever made, but it was a clean hit."

Then there was the play that stopped Packers fullback Jim Taylor just short of the goal line in the Eagles 17–13 win over Green Bay in the 1960 NFL title game—a game in which Bednarik played 58 of the 60 minutes. "That game without a doubt was the greatest game I ever had," Bednarik has since said.

Bednarik retired in 1962 (he had nearly retired twice before, in 1956 and 1959, but was talked out of those) and was inducted into the Pro Football Hall of Fame in 1967. In 1969 he was inducted into the College Football Hall of Fame as well. That same year Bednarik was voted the greatest center of all time by a group of sportswriters, former players, and coaches, and he was named to the All-Time 50 Year NFL team in 1970. He had missed only three games during a career driven by his conviction that every time he stepped on the football field, he was the best there was. "I always played with a certain amount of cockiness," he said. "You must have absolute confidence in football. You must feel like you are the best at your position at all times."

He won't get any argument about that from Eagles fans.

# The Lean Years

Once again change was afoot in the NFL as a new decade began. The New York Bulldogs merged with the Giants. Three new teams joined the league in 1950 as a result of the collapse of the All-American Football Conference (AAFC)—the Cleveland Browns, the San Francisco 49ers, and the Baltimore Colts. And the Eagles would get the pleasure of welcoming the Browns to the NFL by playing Cleveland in the season opener.

It was a pleasure they could have done without. A record crowd of 71,237 fans turned out in Philadelphia to witness their team be embarrassed by the Browns by a score of 35–10. The Browns were led by two future Hall of Famers, running back Marion Motley and quarterback Otto Graham, and had won the AAFC championship four times. This game was a showdown between the champions of the two competing leagues— the defending NFL champion Eagles versus the title bearers from the AAFC—and the game received national attention. It was a disaster for the Eagles and the reputation of the NFL. Graham passed for 346 yards against the Philadelphia defense, while the Eagles could only manage two scores, a 17-yard touchdown pass from Bill Mackrides to Pete Pihos and a 15-yard field goal by Cliff Patton.

Philadelphia bounced back the following week in Chicago in a rematch of the 1947 and 1948 title games, pummeling the Cardinals 45–7. The Eagles defense intercepted eight passes: Russ Craft had four, tying an NFL record, Joe Sutton had another three, and Frank Reagan had one. Two Eagles touchdowns were scored on laterals, including one after a Sutton interception in which he returned the ball 32 yards before flipping it to Reagan, who completed the 79-yard play.

*Pete Retzlaff's Eagles career began to blossom when he was moved from running back to wide receiver, giving quarterback Norm Van Brocklin another viable target in the late 1950s.*

The Eagles would win their next four games for a 5–1 record. They then lost to Pittsburgh 9–7, although they followed that with a 33–0 victory over the Redskins. With a 6–2 record, Philadelphia was on track for another division title, this one in the new American Division, and a trip to the championship game for the fourth straight season. But their hopes were dashed after four straight defeats, including a particularly tough 7–3 loss to the Giants in New York, where the Eagles were stopped from scoring inside the 5-yard line three times. They finished the season with a 6–6 record and a third-place finish in the American Division. Van Buren had an off year, rushing for 629 yards for just a 3.3 yard-per-carry average. He didn't even lead the team as running back—Frank Ziegler did.

This fall from the top was the opening that new owner James P. Clark was looking for in order to take control of the team and get rid of Neale. He fired the legendary Eagles coach with a telegram in February 1951 while Neale was on vacation in Lake Worth, Florida. Bo McMillin, a successful college football coach from Indiana, was hired to replace Neale in 1951. After opening with a 17–14 win over the Cardinals in Chicago and a 21–14 victory over the San Francisco 49ers before a home crowd of more than 23,000 fans, McMillin had to step down when he was diagnosed with stomach cancer. Former Redskins star wide receiver Wayne Millner took over.

By that time the Eagles were in the midst of a great deal of personnel upheaval; their core stars were aging and they were searching for new players to replace them. They won only two of their final 10 games for a 4–8 record. There were some bright moments, however; center Vic Lindskog and linebacker Chuck Bednarik were both named All-Pro, and kicker and end Bobby Walston was named United Press Rookie of the Year. Walston finished fourth in the league in scoring with 94 points on eight touchdowns, six field goals, and 28 extra points.

The team hired its fourth coach in three years at the start of the 1952 season when the owners brought in Wichita coach Jim Trimble, who at age 34 was the youngest head coach in the NFL. Trimble had one player in mind for the 1952 draft to begin his tenure as Eagles coach—a talented black running back out of Drake named Johnny Bright. The team made Bright its number-one pick. But he refused to come to Philadelphia, opting instead to play in the Canadian Football League. A tragic incident during his senior year in a game against Oklahoma A&M

(now Oklahoma State) made Bright wary of the attention he would receive in the NFL. Targeted by the A&M defense because of his race, he was brutally punched and hit by A&M end Wilbanks Smith, coming away with a broken jaw.

The Eagles selected Bright in the first round, ahead of such stars as Frank Gifford and Hugh McElhenny, but Bright just didn't want the attention. Instead he played in relative obscurity in Canada, though he did leave his mark in the CFL, retiring in 1964 as the league's all-time rusher. "I would have been [the Eagles'] first Negro player," Bright said after retiring. "There was a tremendous influx of Southern players into the NFL at that time, and I didn't know what kind of treatment I could expect."

The loss of Bright was a particularly tough blow because the team had hoped he could replace Van Buren, who had suffered a career-ending knee injury—though Trimble would call on Van Buren to be a part of his coaching staff, along with Lindskog, who had retired as well. Trimble made some dramatic personnel moves, playing Pete Pihos almost exclusively at defensive end and replacing him with end Bud Grant—the same Bud Grant who would go on to become a Hall of Fame head coach for the Minnesota Vikings. Trimble also started a new quarterback named Bobby Thomason.

The moves had Eagles fans nervous, but they were calmed by the team's 31–25 opening-game win over the Steelers in Pittsburgh. The team was inconsistent over the next five weeks, with a pattern of winning one and losing one, but finished the season with four victories in its final six games for a 7–5 record and a second-place finish in the American Conference. Thomason finished with eight touchdown passes and completed 95 of 212 attempts for 1,334 yards. More than half of those completions—56 of them—went to Grant, who was the team's offensive star, gaining 997 yards receiving for a 17.8 yard-per-catch average and seven touchdowns, finishing second in the league in receiving. Walston scored 82 points, hit on 11 of 20 field goals, made all 31 extra point attempts, and caught three touchdown passes.

Trimble's team improved to a 7–4–1 mark and achieved another

## TRIVIA

**Which NFL record does Eagles quarterback Adrian Burk share?**

*Answers to the trivia questions are on pages 160–161.*

That Steve Van Buren's brother played for the Eagles? Philadelphia believed they could get lucky twice when they selected Steve's brother, running back Ebert Van Buren, out of LSU in the first round of the 1951 draft. Sadly, Ebert was a bust, gaining a total of only 61 rushing yards, returning two kicks, and intercepting two passes in his three seasons with the team.

second-place finish in the Eastern Conference in 1953. Pihos moved back to offense, catching a league-leading 63 passes for 1,049 yards, and was named All-Pro. Thomason threw 21 touchdown passes, while tackle Vic Sears retired at the end of the season. The 1954 season resulted in a 7–4–1 record (the same as 1953), and a third straight second-place finish in the conference. The owners and fans were getting anxious about taking the next step.

But in 1955 the next step would actually be backward, as the Eagles reversed their record, going 4–7–1 and tying for fourth place in the conference. The team's general manager, Philadelphia Fire Commissioner Frank McNamee, fired Trimble at the end of the season. Pihos ended his brilliant career by leading the league again in catches, with 62—it was the third time he had topped all NFL receivers. He would be inducted into the Pro Football Hall of Fame 15 years later.

The next two seasons were dismal—the Eagles went just 3–8–1 under new coach Hugh Devore in 1956 and followed that up with a 4–8 record in 1957. It got so bad that Bednarik even considered retiring. But there were a few glimmers of hope, including the 1956 debut of talented converted fullback Pete Retzlaff, who caught 12 passes at tight end as a rookie and seemed poised to emerge as one of the league's top players at that position. Tommy McDonald, another end who debuted the following season, would also leave his mark on the franchise. And a young quarterback named Sonny Jurgensen, playing second fiddle to Thomason, seemed to have star quality written all over him. Jurgensen would eventually become a star passer, although his best days would be later in his career, in Washington, D.C.

It would be another quarterback who would lead the Eagles out of the abyss and back to the top, with the help of a new coach as well. Lawrence "Buck" Shaw, who had been a successful coach for the San Francisco 49ers for five years in the NFL with a 33–25–2 record, was hired to coach the Eagles in 1958. His biggest decision was to bring in veteran quarterback Norm Van Brocklin (otherwise known as "the Dutchman"), obtained from the Rams in exchange for guard Buck Lansford, defensive back Jimmy Harris, and a number one draft choice.

Philadelphia fans were not happy with their new coach or their new quarterback in 1958; the team fell to a 2–9–1 record and Van Brocklin threw 20 interceptions. But after a year of adjustment and the emergence of Retzlaff and McDonald as Van Brocklin's primary weapons, things started to click in 1959. The Eagles went 7–5, finishing second in the Eastern Conference and setting the stage for what would be an unforgettable season.

# Champions

Just as in the past, the NFL was facing a challenge from an upstart league, the American Football League (AFL), as the 1950s came to a close. This time, though, they would be facing it without the man who had helped build the NFL into a force on the American sports landscape. Bert Bell passed away of a heart attack at an Eagles-Steelers game—of all places—at Franklin Field in Philadelphia on October 11, 1959, at the age of 64. The league would call on former publicist and general manager of the Los Angeles Rams Pete Rozelle to take them into the new decade.

There was a sense of urgency for the Eagles before the season began because both Shaw and Van Brocklin had announced that they would be retiring at the end of the year. Optimism about the season took a hit, as did the Eagles, in the season opener, as Philadelphia lost to the Browns 41–24 at home before more than 56,000 fans at Franklin Field. They managed to squeeze out a 27–25 win the following week over the league's newest team, the woeful Dallas Cowboys, thanks to two blocked extra points. But the Eagles squad began to get back on track in week three back home against the St. Louis Cardinals—the former Chicago Cardinals after the franchise move—as Van Brocklin threw three touchdown passes in a 31–27 victory.

The Eagles had an easier time in week four, beating the Detroit Lions 28–10, then followed that up by avenging their opening loss to the Browns, going to Cleveland and coming away with a 31–29 win on a 38-yard field goal by Bobby Walston with 10 seconds left in the game. In week six Philadelphia defeated Pittsburgh at home 34–7 to take over first place in the Eastern Conference. But while beating the Redskins 19–13, the Eagles lost their leading rusher, fullback Clarence Peaks, to a broken leg. He would be out for the rest of the season.

The two-way dinosaur, center/linebacker Chuck Bednarik, put the finishing touches on the Eagles' 17–13 NFL championship win over Green Bay in 1960 with a tackle of Packers fullback Jim Taylor nine yards from the goal line as time ran out.

The Eagles faced the Giants, the second-place team and a division rival, in New York the following week. The offense had slowed down with the loss of Peaks, but the defense, led by linebackers Chuck Bednarik and Maxie Baughan and cornerback Tom Brookshier, kept the Eagles on top. It was in this November 20, 1960, contest at Yankee Stadium that Chuck Bednarik created his lasting image in the NFL with the brutal blow that knocked Frank Gifford out of football for a year and a half.

The Eagles would play the Giants again the following week, this time before more than 60,000 fans at Franklin Field. The Eagles won 31–23, spurred on by a defensive effort that boasted four interceptions and a fumble recovery. With two consecutive losses and a 5–3–1 record, the Giants had quickly fallen behind the 8–1 Eagles in the Eastern Conference. Philadelphia clinched the Eastern Division crown in St. Louis on December 4 with a 20–6 victory over the Cardinals.

With so many unknowns ahead, Rozelle could use a memorable season, and he got one. Over in the Western Conference, three weeks before the regular season was scheduled to end, the Green Bay Packers, the Baltimore Colts, and the San Francisco 49ers were all tied for first at 6–4, while the Chicago Bears, at 5–4–1, and the Detroit Lions, at 5–5, were right behind the pack. There was the very real possibility of a four-way tie! But the Packers, led by Coach Vince Lombardi, emerged from the bunch as champions, clinching the Western Conference with a 35–21 win over the Rams.

The Eagles, after winning nine straight, lost to the Steelers 27–21 in Pittsburgh, although they made the meaningless game dramatic. The Steelers had a 27–0 lead going into the fourth; with Jurgensen at quarterback, the Eagles came back to score 21 points with touchdown passes to Tim Brown and Tommy McDonald and a Brown run for a score. Philadelphia finished the season with a 38–28 win over Washington, going into the NFL championship game with a 10–2 record and positive momentum.

The city of Philadelphia was in a frenzy for the game, to be played the day after Christmas. It wasn't televised live in Philadelphia, but was instead

## TRIVIA

How many players on the 1960 Eagles championship team were named to the Pro Bowl?

*Answers to the trivia questions are on pages 160–161.*

71

**All-1950s Team**

| Position | Name |
| --- | --- |
| Coach | Buck Shaw |
| *Offense* | |
| End | Pete Retzlaff |
| | Tommy McDonald |
| Tackle | Lum Snyder |
| | J.D. Smith |
| Guard | Buck Lansford |
| | Stan Campbell |
| Center | Chuck Bednarik |
| Quarterback | Norm Van Brocklin |
| Halfback | Billy Barnes |
| Fullback | Clarence Peaks |
| *Defense* | |
| End | Norm Willey |
| | Tom Scott |
| Tackle | Jess Richardson |
| | Frank "Bucko" Kilroy |
| Linebacker | Chuck Bednarik |
| | Wayne Robinson |
| | Maxie Baughan |
| Cornerback | Tom Brookshier |
| | Jimmy Carr |
| Safety | Don Burroughs |
| | Jerry Norton |
| Kicker | Bobby Walston |
| Punter | Norm Van Brocklin |

taped and replayed at 11:00 PM on local television—so everyone wanted to be there in person for the historic contest. Nearly 7,000 temporary seats were added to Franklin Field to accommodate the crowd of 67,325. The game's attendance set an NFL record for gross receipts at the gate, bringing in $747,876, which resulted in an all-time high for player shares: $5,116 for the winners and $3,105 for the losers.

Philadelphia nearly suffered a disaster early in the first minute when a lateral by Van Brocklin was plucked out of the air by Packer Bill Quinlan for a first down on the Eagles' 14. But the Eagles held the Packers off. Green Bay took a 6–0 lead on two field goals, but in the second quarter Van Brocklin hit Tommy McDonald for a 35-yard touchdown and a 7–6 lead. The Eagles then added a 15-yard Bobby Walston field goal to take a 10–6 lead into halftime. In the fourth quarter Green Bay took the lead again on a seven-yard touchdown pass from Bart Starr to Max McGee. But the Eagles would not be denied; after Ted Dean took the kickoff 58 yards down to the Green Bay 39 following the Packers' touchdown, the Eagles drove down toward the goal line and scored the winning touchdown on a five-yard run by Dean, putting Philadelphia on top for good by the score of 17–13.

Van Brocklin was the hero on offense and was named the game's Most Valuable Player. But Bednarik, at the age of 35, was the true star of the day. With linebacker Bob Pellegrini injured, Bednarik played both ways—center and linebacker—staying in the action for 58 minutes. He knocked Paul Hornung, the league's scoring leader, out of the action with a rib-rattling tackle early in the third quarter. He recovered a fumble that stopped a promising Packer march in the fourth. And when the Packers mounted their last threat, Bednarik tackled fullback Jim Taylor nine yards from the goal line as time expired. "That game without a doubt was the greatest game I ever had," Bednarik said.

# Tommy McDonald:
# A Showman and a Star

Tommy McDonald was a star before he came to Philadelphia. Born in Roy, New Mexico, McDonald was a star athlete at Highland High School in Albuquerque. He continued his winning ways as a standout running back on the legendary Oklahoma Sooners team that won 30 straight games and two national championships under Coach Bud Wilkinson (as part of the Sooners' 47-game winning streak). Despite being only 5'9" and weighing a mere 170 pounds, McDonald rushed for 1,683 yards over three seasons, averaging 6.8 yards per carry, and completed 28 of 44 passes while running the halfback option. He was an All-American and the 1956 winner of the Maxwell Award, given to the college football player of the year. He also came close to being the Heisman Trophy winner, finishing third in a very deep field behind winner (and Notre Dame golden boy) Paul Hornung, as well as Johnny Majors.

McDonald did nothing to disappoint Eagles fans when he arrived as a rookie in 1957—in the seven seasons he played in Philadelphia, he would be named to five Pro Bowls. Because of his small size, he wasn't selected until the third round of the 1957 NFL draft. The Eagles struck gold with that pick. They moved him to wide receiver, where he flourished. When he retired in 1968 McDonald was sixth all-time in receptions, with 495; fourth in yards receiving, with 8,410 (averaging 17 yards per catch); and second in touchdown catches, with 84. Despite his size, McDonald missed only three games in his first 11 years in the league. He caught at least one pass in 93 consecutive games. He also ran back kicks and returned 73 punts for 404 yards (a 5.5 yard average) and one touchdown during his career. He also ran back 51 kickoffs for 1,055 yards—a 20.7 yard average per return.

*Future Hall of Fame players Tommy McDonald (right) and quarterback Sonny Jurgensen watch the action during a game in the early 1960s.*

DID YOU KNOW . . .

That Tommy McDonald might not have been drafted by the Eagles if team management hadn't consulted Bud Wilkinson about the future Pro Bowler? When the Eagles asked Oklahoma coach Wilkinson if his 5'9", 175-pound halfback was big enough to play in the NFL, the Sooners coach replied, "I don't think Tommy is big enough to make it as a running back in the pros. But man, he'd make one excellent flanker." Wilkinson certainly knew what he was talking about.

McDonald was Norm Van Brocklin's go-to receiver. From 1958 to 1962 McDonald caught 58 touchdown passes in 64 games. One of those catches—a 35-yard touchdown reception from Van Brocklin in the 1960 NFL championship game, in which the Eagles defeated the Green Bay Packers 17–13—is an especially great memory for Eagles fans. The Dutchman had the utmost confidence in McDonald. "Most of the time, Tommy doesn't have to run a pass pattern against a defensive back," Van Brocklin once told reporters. "He just beats them."

McDonald's best season may have been the 1961 campaign, with Jurgensen starting for Philadelphia. McDonald led the league in reception yardage, with 1,144 yards, and in touchdown catches, with 13. The 237 yards receiving he had in a December 12 loss to the New York Giants remains a franchise record (he caught seven passes that day, two for touchdowns). When Van Brocklin, who had led the Eagles to the 1960 NFL championship, retired at the end of that season, the story goes that McDonald told Jurgensen, "You just throw the ball. I'll make you just as great a passer as I made Van Brocklin." Jurgensen threw 32 touchdowns that season for 3,723 yards.

But what made McDonald—who made numerous commercials and participated in countless promotions as a player—a favorite of Eagles fans was his love of the spotlight and the attention. He embraced his hero status in a town that is fanatical about its sports. He played with visible enthusiasm in an era when players did not display much emotion on the field, and the fans loved to see it. "He just lives in another world," his Eagles roommate, quarterback Sonny Jurgensen, told reporters.

Sometimes that enthusiasm would have to be tempered. "I used to have to shut him up," Van Brocklin told writers about huddles with McDonald. "But he had a very high percentage of success on the plays he brought back to the huddle."

McDonald was a showman, to say the least. One story claims that in high school he once jumped from a balcony, did a flip, and landed on his feet during a student rally—all while wearing a dress. At Oklahoma he jumped out of a second-floor dorm window to get away from a teammate who had been tricked by McDonald into smearing shaving cream all over his face while sleeping. As an Eagle, McDonald once pretended to have drowned in the training room whirlpool. On another occasion he showed up at a store promotion wearing a dirty uniform—he had forgotten that a mandatory practice was scheduled to run past his appearance time.

McDonald was the last player in the NFL to play without a face mask, and he also played during most of one season with his mouth wired shut because of a broken jaw. For McDonald, the hardest thing about the situation was probably having to keep his mouth shut.

But McDonald never let his exuberant personality get in the way of his play. In fact at Oklahoma, Wilkinson called McDonald "the best halfback I've ever coached." After the Packers lost to the Eagles in the 1960 championship game, legendary Green Bay coach Vince Lombardi declared that if he had 11 Tommy McDonalds on his team, he would never lose.

McDonald was traded to the Dallas Cowboys after the 1963 season, then moved to the Los Angeles Rams the following year. In 1965 he made his sixth and final Pro Bowl appearance and had one of his best seasons, catching 67 passes for 1,036 yards and nine touchdowns. He played his last two years with Atlanta—pulling down 33 passes for 436 yards with the Falcons in 1967—and the Cleveland Browns before he retired.

After the trade to Cleveland, Browns defensive back Bernie Parrish was glad to have McDonald on his side for a change; Parrish had "hated" covering McDonald when they were on opposing teams. Parrish had, he

**DID YOU KNOW . . .** That when Tommy McDonald scored a touchdown, he often put on an end zone act worthy of Chad Johnson or Terrell Owens? He would throw the ball up in the air, dance, and sometimes jump into the arms of his quarterback. While playing for the Rams McDonald once knocked quarterback Bill Munson on his face while trying to jump on his back. "It was the hardest I was hit all afternoon," Munson joked.

said, the "ultimate respect for [McDonald's] great courage and competitive spirit and guts."

That was what Eagles fans loved about Tommy McDonald, and it was always there for them to see. In case anyone forgot the McDonald style, he showed it for everyone once again when he was inducted into the Pro Football Hall of Fame in Canton, Ohio, in 1998. "God Almighty, I feel good!" shouted McDonald as he hit the stage. He then put on a comedy routine, stunning onlookers by tossing his 25-pound bronze bust around as if it were a football. McDonald pulled a radio out of his briefcase and danced to disco music on the steps of the hall while live on national television. He performed chest bumps and high fives with fellow inductees Mike Singletary, Anthony Munoz, Paul Krause, and Dwight Stephenson. "Oh baby!" McDonald shouted. "Do I look excited, like I just won the lottery or the jackpot? Yes! I'm in the Hall of Fame!"

McDonald brought smiles to the faces of the people in the crowd at Canton that day, just as he had for Philadelphia fans for so many years.

# The Abyss

Eagles fans wanted to hang on to the glow of the 1960 NFL championship because there was so much uncertainty looming over the team going into the 1961 season. Their coach, Buck Shaw, had retired, as had one of the team leaders, quarterback Norm Van Brocklin. Philadelphia fans were not oblivious to the fact that it was Shaw and Van Brocklin who had pulled the team out of its habitual mediocrity.

Reportedly, there was a deal in place for Van Brocklin to take over as the Eagles coach after he retired. Instead management hired Nick Skorich, creating turmoil throughout the organization and unsettling the fans in the process. Skorich, however, quickly did what needed to be done to win the fans over—he won games. The team opened the season with two straight wins at home, a 27–20 victory over the Cleveland Browns and a 14–7 win against the Washington Redskins. After a 30–27 loss to the Cardinals, the Eagles went on to win five straight.

Jurgensen had a standout season, stepping in as the starter and throwing 32 touchdown passes and a league-record 3,723 yards. Tommy McDonald caught 64 passes for 1,144 yards and 13 touchdowns, earning a place in the Pro Bowl. Pete Retzlaff continued as a dominant tight end, catching 50 passes for 769 yards and eight touchdowns. Running back Timmy Brown emerged as the team's most versatile and reliable offensive weapon, averaging 6.8 yards per carry while rushing for 338 yards and catching 14 passes for 264 yards, an 18.9 yard-per-catch average.

With the Eastern Conference title at stake, the Eagles went into their 13th game facing the New York Giants at home; they lost 28–24 despite a strong performance from Jurgensen, who threw for 367 yards and three touchdowns. They finished the season with a 10–4 record, good enough for second place in the conference. It wasn't quite the NFL championship, but an appearance in the Playoff Bowl—a game featuring the runners-up in each conference—did at least create the appearance that the franchise had made a smooth transition and would continue its winning ways (despite a 38–10 loss to the Detroit Lions in that consolation contest). However, the game took a heavy toll on the Eagles: Jurgensen suffered a shoulder separation that would affect his play in the 1962 season, and Pro Bowl offensive tackle J.D. Smith suffered a broken leg.

Fans still bought into what the Eagles were selling: the franchise sold more than 44,000 season tickets in 1962. Those fans would wind up a sorely disappointed bunch. Skorich got rid of a number of older veterans, including Ed Khayat, Sam Baker, and Bob Pellegrini, and went with a youth movement—but it got old pretty quickly. They won only one of their first 10 games, defeating the Cleveland Browns 35–7 to deliver one win for the home crowd of 60,671. The Eagles would manage only two more victories, both near the end of the season, and finished the year with a 3–10–1 mark. The season's disappointments included a 49–0 shutout by the Green Bay Packers, the team they had beaten in the NFL title game two years prior. Jurgensen threw for 22 touchdowns, but also had 26 interceptions. Chuck Bednarik retired at the end of the season.

Brown proved to be a diamond in the rough, rushing for 545 yards, catching 52 passes for 849 yards, and scoring a total of 11 touchdowns. He also led the team with 831 yards in kickoff-return yardage, a 27.7-yard average, with one 99-yard return for a score.

Team owner James Clark passed away during the season, and the team was put up for sale. One of the prospective buyer groups was very unique—they already had full-time jobs as president, attorney general, and senator. John, Robert, and Ted Kennedy considered buying the franchise, but other things—such as the Cuban Missile Crisis—got in the way, and the Kennedy bid stalled in the exploratory stage.

The bad times continued in 1963, with a 2–10–2 record. The first of the two victories came in a close, 24–21, game against Dallas. The only other bright spot came when the Eagles beat the Redskins 37–24, a game in which Jurgensen threw four touchdown passes for 315 yards. McDonald caught two of those passes; Brown caught another and ran for a third score.

Soon after that, the team was engulfed in a storm of turmoil and controversy. The day after President Kennedy was assassinated, word came from Commissioner Pete Rozelle that the Eagles would have to play that Sunday. A team meeting about the issue resulted in a brutal locker room brawl between cornerback Ben Scotti and defensive tackle John Mellekas. Scotti reportedly objected to an ethnic slur made by defensive end Bill Quinlan about Rozelle, at which point Mellekas jumped up and picked a fight with Scotti. The two went to another room where, as the story goes, Scotti nearly beat Mellekas senseless. Both men had to be hospitalized: Mellekas suffered a broken nose, a black eye, and left several teeth on the floor in a pool of blood; Scotti had severe cuts to the tendons of his hands

*In 1969 Leonard Tose bought the Eagles franchise for a then-record $16.1 million.*

caused by knocking those teeth out of Mellekas's mouth. "I let out all my anger of the whole year and everything else out on him," Scotti told *New York Post* columnist Milton Gross. "I knocked him down, and I stood over him and worked him over." Scotti was released by the team, and Mellekas was fined $500. He retired at the end of the season.

The front office was also a mess. After the season, the team was sold to a Washington businessman named Jerry Wolman, who paid $5.5 million for the club and then hired Coach Joe Kuharich, formerly with the Cardinals and the Redskins, to a lifetime contract. In reality Kuharich would last only five years, but it seemed like a lifetime to Eagles fans. One of the new coach's first moves was to trade quarterback Sonny Jurgensen to the Redskins in exchange for Norm Snead. Jurgensen would go on to have a Hall of Fame career in Washington, while Snead had a very ordinary NFL career.

No one was complaining, however, after Kuharich's coaching debut in week one of the 1964 season at Franklin Field. The reorganized Eagles beat the Giants for the first time since 1960 by a score of 38–7. New fullback Earl Gros ran 59 yards for a touchdown on the first play from scrimmage. Snead threw two touchdown passes, one to Retzlaff, who gained 139 yards on six catches, and the second to Brown, who scored twice. Free safety Don Burroughs sacked Giants quarterback Y.A. Tittle five times on safety blitzes.

But while the team managed to improve in the standings, they still finished with a losing record, going 6–8 and tying for third in the Eastern Conference. One of those losses, a particularly painful one for Philadelphia fans, saw Jurgensen throw for 385 yards and five touchdown passes in a 35–20 Redskins win in Washington, D.C.

Wolman made news before the start of the 1965 season when, during an exhibition game against the Redskins at the Eagles' training camp in Hershey, Pennsylvania, he and assistant coach Fred Bruney came out of the press box and got into a fight with some Redskins fans who had been heckling the Eagles throughout the game. According to a story in *The Philadelphia Inquirer*, fans scattered as the fight moved through several rows of seats. The fans might have enjoyed getting a shot at Wolman and Bruney themselves.

The team did give hometown fans something to cheer for in the season opener, beating the St. Louis Cardinals 34–27 for the first time since 1961. Two long kickoff returns—a 70-yarder by rookie Al Nelson and a 74-yarder by Irv Cross to open the second half—led to Eagles scores. Timmy Brown caught seven passes for 129 yards and a touchdown out of the backfield. These winning ways were short-lived, however, as the team won only four more times that year for a 5–9 record, tying for fifth place in the Eastern Conference.

Suddenly, though, it all seemed to click in 1966. After losing their opener 16–13 to the Cardinals in St. Louis, the Eagles went on to win nine of their next 13 games. The most memorable win came when Philadelphia, avenging an earlier 56–7 loss to the Cowboys, defeated Dallas 24–23 at home, with all points scored by special teams. Brown became the first player in NFL history to return two kickoffs for touchdowns in the same game, with a 93-yard runback in the first quarter and a 90-yarder in the second quarter. Aaron Martin put the Eagles ahead in the second quarter with a 67-yard punt return for a touchdown. Sam Baker, back with Philadelphia, also kicked a 31-yard field goal. The team tied for second in the Eastern Conference and played in another Playoff Bowl, losing 20–14 to the Baltimore Colts.

To fans, 1966 must have seemed like just a tease when the Eagles finished the 1967 season with another losing record, going 6–7–1. It became the first team to lose to the expansion New Orleans franchise, dropping a 31–24 game to the Saints, and star offensive tackle Bob Brown was lost for the season with an injury.

Then the bottom fell out. In 1968 the Eagles had one of their worst seasons in recent franchise memory, going only 2–12. One of the few positives for Eagles fans that season was the arrival of flakey defensive end/linebacker Tim Rossovich, who set his hair on fire, chewed broken glass, and hit hard on the field. But it was not enough of a distraction; the fans blamed Kuharich for the team's dismal performance, and their demands that "Joe Must Go" were getting too loud to ignore.

Those demands would finally be met by new owner Leonard Tose. Tose had actually been a part of the "Happy Hundred," the group of investors led by James P. Clark that had purchased the team back in 1949. This time around he acquired the franchise for $16.1 million in bankruptcy court when Wolman faced financial problems.

Tose inherited one of those financial problems in the form of Joe Kuharich, who had received a stunning 15-year contract from Wolman.

All-1960s Team

| Position | Name |
|----------|------|
| Coach | No worthy candidates |
| *Offense* | |
| End | Ben Hawkins |
| | Harold Jackson |
| Tight End | Pete Retzlaff |
| Tackle | Bob Brown |
| | Dave Graham |
| Guard | Ed Blaine |
| | Jim Skaggs |
| Center | Jim Ringo |
| Quarterback | Norm Snead |
| Halfback | Tim Brown |
| Fullback | Tom Woodeshick |
| *Defense* | |
| End | Tim Rossovich |
| | Mel Tom |
| Tackle | Floyd Peters |
| | Gary Pettigrew |
| Linebacker | Dave Lloyd |
| | Maxie Baughan |
| | Chuck Bednarik |
| Cornerback | Irv Cross |
| | Al Nelson |
| Safety | Bill Bradley |
| | Nate Ramsey |
| Kicker | Sam Baker |
| Returner | Tim Brown |

Tose was forced to keep paying Kuharich—who received a total of $900,000 over the life of the contract—for 11 more years. Tose nevertheless fired Kuharich and replaced him with Jerry Williams, a former Eagles player and successful Canadian Football League coach; the team improved slightly in Williams's first season in 1969, going 4–9–1 and finishing fourth (last place) in the Capitol Division.

Part of the improvement was because of the key trade of running back Izzy Lang to the Rams for receiver Harold Jackson, who led the team with 65 catches for 1,116 yards and nine touchdowns, becoming a franchise star. Still, Philadelphia fans were glad to say good-bye to the 1960s, which had seemed so promising in the beginning. Everyone thought the 1970s would be better. For the most part, they were wrong.

# A Familiar Pattern

First there was the opening 17–7 loss to the Dallas Cowboys before 59,728 angry Eagles fans. Then there was the 20–16 loss to the Bears in Chicago, followed by the 33–21 defeat at the hands of the Redskins. Next there was a 30–23 loss to the Giants in New York.

A pattern of losing had carried over from the previous decade, and Jerry Williams's squad showed no signs of changing that pattern, finishing the 1970 season with a 3–10–1 record. The merger between the NFL and the American Football League took effect in 1970, a year after Joe Namath and the New York Jets upset the Baltimore Colts in Super Bowl III. The league was reorganized into two 13-team conferences (National and American), and the Eagles became part of the five-team NFC East. They finished last in their first year in the new division.

It was also the first year for *Monday Night Football,* and the Eagles at least had a winning debut, defeating the New York Giants at home 23–20 on November 23 before a crowd of 59,117 Eagles fans. Halfback Cyril Pinder carried the ball 19 times for 89 yards, end Ben Hawkins caught four passes for 99 yards, and Tim Rossovich led the defense.

The team also gave Franklin Field a proper farewell when they beat the Pittsburgh Steelers 30–20 on December 20, the final regular-season game at the stadium. In his last game as an Eagle, Norm Snead completed 21 of 29 passes for 276 yards with two touchdowns and two interceptions. He was traded to Minnesota after the season.

In 1971 the Eagles moved into their new home, Veterans Stadium— one of the many cookie-cutter, multipurpose stadiums that were erected during the same period, along with Three Rivers Stadium in Pittsburgh and Riverfront Stadium in Cincinnati. As with those facilities, Veterans would house both baseball and football, in this case the Eagles and the city's baseball team, the Phillies.

The Eagles went into the season with Canadian import Pete Liske at quarterback—definitely their Plan B as far as that position was concerned. Needing a new quarterback following the trade of Snead to Minnesota, the Eagles had traded three draft picks (the highest being a second-round choice) to the Lions for Greg Barton, a third-string quarterback who had thrown only one pass in the NFL. Barton promptly signed with the Toronto Argonauts of the CFL instead, leaving Philadelphia scrambling for a quarterback.

After losing the 1971 season opener in Cincinnati 37–14, the Eagles christened their new home with a 42–7 loss to the Cowboys before 65,358 fans, then followed that with a 31–3 defeat at the hands of the San Francisco 49ers. With three losses for a combined score of 110–24 to start the season, owner Leonard Tose—like the fans—had seen enough. Coach Williams was fired. Williams ripped Tose for his decision and, despite their record, the players were loyal to Williams and nearly revolted against Tose.

Defensive line coach Ed Khayat took over. The team responded to his disciplinarian style, finishing the season 6–2–1 for an overall mark of 6–7–1 and a third-place finish in the NFC East. A strong defense pulled the team through, giving up 302 points as the offense scored only 221. The defense was led by safety Bill Bradley, the Eagles' only Pro Bowl selection, who had 11 interceptions and 248 yards on the return of those picks.

With the team's strong finish, Eagles fans once again had high hopes going into 1972. Those hopes were quickly dashed. After a 28–6 opening-game loss to the Cowboys in Dallas and a 27–17 defeat by Cleveland at home, the grumbling among the media and fans was so great that Tose guaranteed his team would beat the Giants in week three on *Monday Night Football*. With the town buzzing about Tose's vow and a national television audience tuning in, the 27–12 defeat to the Giants seemed that much worse; it was compounded by the fact that former quarterback Snead, now playing for New York, threw three touchdown passes. Philadelphia would manage only two wins that season and nearly went all year without a victory, as both of their wins were by a margin of only one point—21–20

# TRIVIA

**During which year did the Eagles have no Pro Bowl representative?**

*Answers to the trivia questions are on pages 160–161.*

over the Kansas City Chiefs and 18–17 against the Houston Oilers. Eagles fans were robbed of watching either victory, however, because both came on the road.

Fans were at least spared hosting the worst loss of the season, a 62–10 beating by the Giants. The season ended with the Eagles holding a 2–11–1 record. The offense, led by rookie quarterback John Reaves, was one of the worst in the history of the franchise, scoring a total of only 145 points. Remarkably, Harold Jackson rose above the mess to catch 62 passes for 1,048 yards and made the Pro Bowl. Khayat was fired, along with general manager Pete Retzlaff, an Eagles legend.

Tose hired Mike McCormack as his new coach for the 1973 season. McCormack was not about to leave his job security in the hands of a young, untested quarterback, so he made several trades to improve the offense. The biggest was acquiring veteran quarterback Roman Gabriel from the Los Angeles Rams. But McCormack paid a steep price for that deal, trading Jackson, running back Tony Baker, two number one draft choices, and a third-round choice. Jackson continued his winning ways as a star receiver with the Rams. Gabriel would pay immediate dividends, but at the age of 33, and having taken a lot of punishment over the years, he was on the downside of his career. McCormack did reap the rewards of a banner draft, starting three rookies who would go on to become Pro Bowl selections: tight end Charle Young, tackle Jerry Sisemore, and center Guy Morriss. He also put Harold Carmichael in the starting lineup, the beginning of Carmichael's run as the franchise's all-time receiver.

It took a while for the new offense to mesh. The Eagles suffered a disappointing opening-game loss to the St. Louis Cardinals in a close, 24–23 game before 61,103 jaded but hopeful fans at Veterans Stadium, and went 0–3–1 in their first four games. McCormack got his first win on October 14, a 27–13 victory over the Cardinals in St. Louis, as Gabriel passed for 379 yards and three touchdowns, including the winning strike to rookie Don Zimmerman on the game's final play, and Carmichael caught 12 passes for 187 yards and two touchdowns. After losing 28–21 to the Minnesota Vikings, the Eagles came back the following week to

*Hard-nosed quarter-back Roman Gabriel came to Philadelphia from the Rams in 1973 and completed 23 touchdown passes. But he couldn't overcome the lack of talent that plagued the franchise during the 1960s and mid-1970s.*

**IF ONLY . . .** Mark Moseley had done all his incredible kicking—263 field goals and 417 extra points—for the Eagles. Moseley, a two-time Pro Bowl player who was named NFL Most Valuable Player in 1982, was one of the Eagles' greatest divisional opponents when he played with the Redskins from 1974 to 1986. He was drafted by Philadelphia in the 14th round in 1970, and beat out veteran Sam Baker to start. Moseley scored 67 points, hitting 14 of 25 field goals and 25 of 28 extra points. He was cut the next season in favor of Happy Feller.

delight the Veterans Stadium faithful with a 30–16 upset over the Dallas Cowboys, their first victory over them in six years. Gabriel threw two touchdown passes to Carmichael and also scored on a quarterback sneak.

Philadelphia ended up with a 5–8–1 record. The changes made to the offense paid off, with the squad doubling its point total from the year before, scoring 310 points. Gabriel brought the passing game back, with 23 touchdowns and 3,219 yards passing and was named NFL Comeback Player of the Year. Carmichael caught 67 passes for 1,116 yards and nine touchdowns, while Young pulled down 55 catches for 854 yards and six touchdowns. Both made the Pro Bowl, as did Gabriel.

But the defense kept them from becoming a winning team, giving up 393 points. The team made a big move to bolster the defense by acquiring linebacker Bill Bergey from the Cincinnati Bengals. It was an important deal for the Eagles; Bergey would become the face of the franchise for the rest of the decade, and was named team Most Valuable Player three times. But again, the move cost them two first-round picks and a second-round choice, and the lack of draft choices would keep the Eagles stuck in mediocrity.

Bergey's presence had an immediate impact on the defense in 1974; the unit held opponents to only 217 points, a dramatic improvement. And they played hard-nosed football, as evidenced by a brawling 31–24 loss to the Cowboys on October 20 in Dallas that saw 12 fights break out on the field. Earlier in the season the defense had been responsible for a 13–10 victory over the Cowboys on *Monday Night Football* when cornerback Joe Lavender recovered a Dallas fumble and returned it 96 yards for a touchdown. A 45-yard field goal by Tom Dempsey with 25 seconds left to play won the game.

Now it was the offense that was struggling, scoring only 40 points over a five-game stretch in the middle of the season. Rookie quarterback Mike Boryla started the last three games, leading the team to wins over Green Bay (36–14), the New York Giants (20–7), and the Detroit Lions (28–17) as the Eagles finished 7–7, fourth in the NFC East.

In what had become an all-too-familiar pattern for Eagles fans, the 1975 season seemed to start with a step back rather than a step forward. Neither Gabriel nor Boryla were effective at quarterback, and this time around the defense could not carry the inept offense. The team went 4–10, landing in fifth place in the NFC East.

A loss in a *Monday Night Football* game at Veterans Stadium on November 3 seemed to bring an end to McCormack's tenure. The Rams, led by quarterback James Harris with three touchdown passes, embarrassed Philadelphia 42–3. Though they won their final game of the year 26–3 over the Redskins, McCormack was gone. Tose was determined to find someone to lead the franchise out of the quicksand it seemed to have been stuck in for the past 15 years. He needed a winner to change the culture of losing—and he would find one.

# Promises of a Super Bowl: The Arrival of Dick Vermeil

When Philadelphia Eagles owner Leonard Tose introduced his new coach—his fourth in seven years—on February 8, 1976, he made a promise to fans: "I don't want to put our other coaches down, but I am telling you that this time, the Philadelphia fans are getting the real thing: a great coach."

Big deal. Eagles fans had heard that before.

But when former UCLA coach Dick Vermeil spoke to reporters, he made a promise that even startled Eagles observers—a Super Bowl commitment. "In five years, the Eagles will be Super Bowl material," Vermeil declared.

Then he went about doing what he needed to do to fulfill that promise. First he set out to change the culture of losing that had dominated the franchise for so long. His training camps were demanding, and those players who didn't go along with the program were gone. He also brought in players who fit his winning ideals. There was one in particular who would help take the franchise to the next level: quarterback Ron Jaworski. But Jaworski did not arrive until a 1977 trade brought him to Philadelphia from Los Angeles. So while Vermeil waited to get his man at quarterback, he suffered through his first season—along with Eagles fans—with a combination of Boryla and Gabriel at quarterback. He lost his debut in Dallas to the Cowboys 27–7, then earned his first victory with a 20–7 win the following week against the New York Giants before the home fans.

There would be only three more victories that season for the Eagles, who had the same record from the year before, going 4–10. Despite this disappointing performance, there were important victories off the field: through his knowledge of the college game, and with the help of general manager Carl Peterson's resourceful drafting, Vermeil began to put together a roster of talented players with winning attitudes. They selected unknown defensive end Carl Hairston from the equally unknown University of Maryland–Eastern Shore in the seventh round in 1976, and in the sixth round in 1977 they found a running back from Abilene Christian named Wilbert Montgomery. Both would go on to be All-Pros and among the best ever to play for the Eagles.

With Jaworski at the helm going into the 1977 season, there was some cautious optimism. The team opened the season with a 13–3 win over the Tampa Bay Buccaneers, but won only two of its next 11 games. Vermeil's crew finished the season with a flourish at home, beating the Giants 17–14, followed by a 27–0 victory over the New York Jets—a noteworthy game because it was the first time Eagles fans got to see much of

*Dick Vermeil came from UCLA, where he had a successful college career, to coach the Eagles in 1976. He made the bold prediction that in five years his team would be "Super Bowl material." Five years later, the Eagles were in the Super Bowl.*

DID YOU KNOW . . . That defensive end Blenda Gay, who had been an integral part of an improving Eagles defense in 1976 under new coach Dick Vermeil, was stabbed to death by his wife after the 1976 season?

Montgomery, who rushed for 103 yards on 22 carries. Meanwhile, Bill Bergey continued to be the defensive mainstay through the tough times, the only player on the Eagles squad selected to the Pro Bowl. Eventually he would be rewarded for his efforts.

It didn't seem as if that reward was on the horizon when the Eagles opened the 1978 season with two straight losses. But they improved quickly, winning four out of their next five contests, the key victory coming on October 15 before 65,722 fans at Veterans Stadium. The mighty Redskins, under new coach Jack Pardee, had come into town with an undefeated 6–0 record, and were heavy favorites to beat the 4–3 Eagles. But the Philadelphia defense stepped up their game, recovering four fumbles and intercepting two passes, and Montgomery rushed for 125 yards, giving the team a 17–10 victory. It would be a key win, and one Philadelphia would need later when it came time to qualify for the wild-card playoff berth.

After going 2–2 in their next four games, the Eagles could not afford to slip into losing—not when there was talk of finally making the playoffs for the first time since 1960. But on November 19 at Giants Stadium they were on their way to a 17–12 defeat after playing a terrible game with two missed extra points and three interceptions thrown by Jaworski, including one with 31 seconds left in the game that seemed to seal the win for New York. No one was prepared for "the Miracle of the Meadowlands" that happened next. Instead of falling on the ball, New York quarterback Joe Pisarcik needlessly handed off to fullback Larry Csonka, who fumbled. Cornerback Herman Edwards picked it up and—to the horror of Giants fans to this day—ran 26 yards for a touchdown and a 19–17 Eagles victory.

Still, the Eagles were inconsistent enough to lose two of their next three games, including a 31–13 loss to the Cowboys in Philadelphia, which meant the final game of the season—also played at Veterans Stadium—might have decided the Eagles' postseason fate. Appropriately, it was against the Giants, and Montgomery rushed for 130 yards on 25 carries and two touchdowns for a 20–3 Eagles victory, beating out the Redskins for the wild card and finishing with a 9–7 mark.

Vermeil had given Eagles fans some true reason for hope—in his third season he had brought them to the playoffs. But the joy of playing in a post-season game was watered down by the Eagles' 14–13 loss to the Atlanta Falcons, mainly because it was a game Philadelphia could have won. The Eagles led 13–0 going into the fourth quarter after a 13-yard touchdown pass from Jaworski to Carmichael and a one-yard touchdown run by Montgomery. But kicker Mike Michel, filling in for an injured Nick Mike-Mayer, missed the extra point after the Carmichael touchdown catch, a mistake that would play a big role in the game. The Falcons came back to score two fourth-quarter touchdowns to take a 14–13 lead. With less than two minutes left, Jaworski hit end Oren Middlebrook on a long pass play that could have been a game-winner—if Middlebrook had caught it. Then Michel missed a 34-yard field goal on the final play of the game.

The Eagles ended the 1978 season hungry, ready to take another step toward fulfilling Vermeil's Super Bowl promise. Jaworski had emerged as a dependable passer, getting his interceptions down to at least equal his touchdown passes—16—for the first time in his career. Montgomery rushed for 1,220 yards, averaging 4.7 yards per carry. And Carmichael continued to be a reliable target, catching 55 passes for 1,072 yards and eight touchdowns. The improvement in the team's talent was reflected by the fact that four Eagles—Bergey, Montgomery, Carmichael, and tackle Stan Walters—made the Pro Bowl.

The team that took the field for the opener at Veterans in 1979 was a totally different squad from the one Vermeil had when he started. In addition to all the other changes, they had also added another young player, Jerry Robinson, who would become one of their best linebackers. The well-balanced Eagles opened with a 23–17 win over the New York Giants before 67,366 fans. They lost a rematch of the wild-card game the year before against the Falcons at home, 14–10, but then won five games in a row, the biggest victory being a 17–14 win at home over the defending Super Bowl champion Pittsburgh Steelers.

After losing three straight (to Washington and Cincinnati on the road and Cleveland at home by a total score

## TRIVIA

**Who is the franchise leader in 100-yard rushing games?**

*Answers to the trivia questions are on pages 160–161.*

of 78–39), there was some concern that these were the same old Eagles who always found a way to fall back when it appeared they were ready to move forward. But now they finally had the talent they needed to sustain a winning season. After defeating the Cowboys in Dallas 31–21 in a game where barefoot kicker Tony Franklin booted the second-longest field goal in NFL history, a 59-yarder, the Eagles went on to win five of their last six games for an 11–5 record, a second-place finish in the NFC East, and another trip to the playoffs.

This time Philadelphia moved closer to their Super Bowl goal—and the hometown fans got to watch it live—as the Eagles defeated the Chicago Bears 27–17 in a December 23 wild-card playoff game at Veterans Stadium. Chicago led 17–10 at halftime after two Walter Payton touchdowns and a field goal, and nearly took a 24–10 lead when Payton ran 84 yards for a touchdown, only to have the play called back on a penalty. But Jaworski showed his leadership by throwing three touch-down passes, including the game-winner, a screen play to halfback Billy Campfield that went for 63 yards.

The next step was going to Tampa to face the Buccaneers in an NFC divisional playoff contest. Again, Philadelphia found itself down early in the game, only this time it was 17–0 in the second quarter. The Eagles had a tough time coming back, as Tampa running back Ricky Bell carried the ball 38 times for 142 yards, scoring two touchdowns and dominating possession time. The Eagles fought hard; Jaworski threw touchdown passes to Carmichael and Charlie Smith, getting Philadelphia to within seven points. But they failed to convert on fourth down with 43 seconds left in the game, and their season came to an end without going on to the next step.

However, in the season to come, Vermeil—who was named NFL Coach of the Year—was about to see his Super Bowl promises become a reality.

# The Polish Rifle Comes to Philly: Ron Jaworski Joins the Eagles

When Ron Jaworski first arrived at the Philadelphia Eagles training camp in 1977, he thought he had landed in a war zone. "When I first got to Philadelphia, I found a bunch of guys shell-shocked from losing," Jaworski said. "They had been through some lean years. They just didn't know what it was like to have fun in football. They were quiet and kept to themselves. I said, 'Hey, this has got to change.' I went around patting guys on the back, telling them everything was going to be cool. It was time for the Eagles to become winners."

Teammates didn't know at first how to react to Jaworski's enthusiasm. "I thought he was crazy," said tackle Stan Walters. "He had this goofy porkpie hat on, and he was yapping away a mile a minute. Every other quarterback I had played with had been a loner or very businesslike. Jaworski wasn't like that. He was laughing and yelling and telling us we're going to be winners. We're coming off a 4–10 record, and he's talking about winning a title. Crazy."

But Ron Jaworski wasn't crazy. He just had a very grounded perspective. He knew how fortunate he and his teammates were to be playing in the NFL. He knew there were people with far more weight on their shoulders in all walks of life. He knew about the power of wanting something and working for it, and he used that power and desire to help his team go from being losers to winning the NFC championship in 1980 and going to the Super Bowl for the first time in franchise history.

He learned all of this from his parents, William and Molly Jaworski, in a steel town called Lackawanna, not far from Buffalo in western New York. Jaworski was a standout athlete at Lackawanna High School, playing football, basketball, and baseball. He had a rifle arm—his

DID YOU KNOW . . .

That Ron Jaworski wasn't the first professional athlete to be nicknamed "the Polish Rifle"? Connie Wisniewski was a star pitcher in the All-American Girls Professional Baseball League with the Milwaukee and Grand Rapid Chicks. She went 32–11 in 1945 and 33–9 in 1946. Born in Detroit, Michigan, Wisniewski was the first "Polish Rifle."

nickname years later would be "the Polish Rifle"—and was scouted by professional baseball as well as football.

Jaworski was drafted out of high school by baseball's St. Louis Cardinals and wanted to take the contract. But William Jaworski wanted his son to go to college. "My dad worked in a lumberyard and he wanted something better for me," Jaworski said. "But you know how teenagers are. All I could see was a Major League career. When you're 17 years old, your idea of preparing for the future is looking at next week."

But Jaworski's father didn't only order his son to go to college, he taught him a valuable lesson. "The summer before my senior year in high school, he had me go to work in the steel mill," Jaworski said. "My job was straightening rods. Pull out a crooked rod, put it in the straightening machine. Pull out another crooked rod, put another one in. After a week I wanted out. He made me stay for two more weeks, just to make sure I got the point."

Jaworski went to play football at nearby Youngstown State in Ohio and was drafted by the Los Angeles Rams in the second round of the 1973 draft. He spent his first season on the team's taxi squad and was added to the roster as backup quarterback in 1974. He saw very little action in Los Angeles, appearing in only a handful of games over three years and completing 54 out of 124 passes for only one touchdown and a dismal eight interceptions.

In 1977 Jaworski was traded by the Rams to the Eagles for tight end Charle Young. There was some controversy about the deal, since both players had completed their contracts and, technically, the trade was illegal, but the league decided to allow it. It was a change that, along with the arrival of new coach Vermeil, opened the door to an era of winning for the Eagles.

Interceptions remained a problem for Jaworski at first, but he showed improvement with each season after arriving in Philadelphia. In

*Quarterback Ron Jaworski came to the Eagles in 1977 and soon became the face of the franchise. He played 10 years in Philadelphia, leading the Eagles to the NFC playoffs four times.*

DID YOU KNOW . . .

That not everyone is a Jaworski fan? Perhaps no Eagle has made more of their post-NFL career than Ron Jaworski. He is an ESPN analyst, a public speaker, and a businessman who owns golf courses and hotels. But not everyone in Philadelphia has been a fan of Jaworski the businessman. When he took over the Holiday Inn near the sports complex, he clashed with the Local 274 Hotel Employees and Restaurant Employees Union, which felt that the former Eagles quarterback fired too many union workers with too little reason. It got so out of hand that a banner saying "Ron Jaworski is a jerk, put 70 people out of work" was seen at games at Veterans Stadium.

1977 he completed 166 of 346 passes for 2,183 yards and threw 18 touchdown passes and 21 interceptions. He was even more in control in 1978, completing 206 of 398 passes for 2,487 yards, 18 touchdowns, and 18 interceptions. He reversed the touchdown-to-interception ratio in 1979, throwing 18 touchdowns while giving up only 12 interceptions.

It was in 1980 that Jaworski had his career year, completing 257 of 451 passes for 3,529 yards and 27 touchdowns with only 12 interceptions, taking the Eagles into Super Bowl XV. He made the Pro Bowl that season and was also named United Press International's NFL Player of the Year. He also won the Bert Bell Award, the Maxwell Football Club's Professional Player of the Year Award, and the Dunlop Tire company's Professional Athlete of the Year Award.

Jaworski had become the face of the Eagles franchise and a Philadelphia fixture. He was known to fans as "Jaws," a nickname given to him by his next-door neighbor Doug Collins, a future NBA coach and television analyst who was a guard at the time for the Philadelphia 76ers. "He didn't come up with Jaws because of that shark movie, though," Jaworski said. "Dougie said it was because my mouth was always open, talking."

Jaworski suffered a broken leg at St. Louis during the 13th game of the 1984 season; by that time he had started in 116 straight games, a record for most consecutive starts. He held that record until 1999, when it was broken by Brett Favre. In 10 years with the Eagles, Jaworski's career statistics included 2,088 completions, 26,963 passing yards, and 175 touchdowns. He led the Eagles to the NFC playoffs four times and is the all-time Eagles leader in many passing categories, including career touchdowns and career passing yardage.

After becoming a free agent in March 1987, Jaworski was signed by the Miami Dolphins, where he played in 1987 and 1988. In 1989 he signed as a free agent with the Kansas City Chiefs. He then retired in 1990 after sustaining a season-ending knee injury.

Since retiring Jaworski has been very active in both football, as a respected analyst for ESPN, and in the community. He was inducted into the National Polish-American Hall of Fame in 1991 and joined the Philadelphia Eagles Honor Roll in 1992. In 1997 he received the Pinnacle Award from the South Jersey Chamber of Commerce for his outstanding volunteer work and longtime service to the chamber and the business community. In 1997 he received the Bert Bell Award from the charitable "Eagles Fly for Leukemia" organization, an award given to individuals who contribute significantly to the NFL, and the following year he was honored by the United Way with their Volunteer Leadership Award, the highest award given by the United Way. Jaworski also introduced a new football franchise to Philadelphia fans as team president of the Philadelphia Soul, the Arena Football League franchise owned by rock star Jon Bon Jovi.

Jaworski's work after football is important to note because, in an era in which athletes are often seen to fall short as role models, he continues to represent the Eagles franchise with pride and hard work off the field.

# The Road to the Super Bowl

The Eagles had made progress every season since the arrival of Dick Vermeil in 1976, and there was only one place left to go in 1980: to New Orleans for Super Bowl XV.

The team was intact for the most part from the previous season. Among the few new faces was the team's number one draft choice, standout rookie cornerback Roynell Young, who earned a starting job. And there was a humorous new name on the roster as a backup quarterback—Joe Pisarcik, of the infamous "Miracle of the Meadowlands" fumble two years earlier with the Giants.

Ron Jaworski was at the top of his game for the season opener at home before a rabid crowd of 70,307, throwing three touchdown passes and completing 19 of 29 attempts for 281 yards, no interceptions, and a 27–6 victory over the Denver Broncos. The second week, in a 42–7 victory over the Minnesota Vikings, running back Wilbert Montgomery was the star, carrying the ball 20 times for 169 yards and two touchdowns, including a career-best 72-yard jaunt. And Jaworski again was almost flawless, completing 20 of 26 passes for 234 yards, two touchdowns, and no interceptions.

The Eagles were a prime-time attraction, putting on quite a show for the country on *Monday Night Football* on September 22 at the Vet, with a frenzied home crowd of 70,767 on hand. Jaworski threw three touchdown passes and his first interception of the season; Harold Carmichael caught six passes, for 111 yards and two touchdowns, in the 35–3 beating of the Giants. In three games Jaworski had thrown eight touchdown passes, and the offense had scored a total of 104 points.

But there were two sides to this unfolding story—the defense, led by veteran linebacker Bill Bergey, was equally impressive, holding its first three opponents to a total of only 16 points. The defense had developed its own identity as a hard-hitting unit. "We hear that leather pop and we get all excited," said linebacker Frank LeMaster. "We're like sharks in a feeding frenzy. Bergey strikes, and the rest of us go wild."

There was nothing wild about the Eagles' fourth game of the season—except Jaworski's passing, which was quite erratic. He passed for one touchdown and ran for another score, but also threw three interceptions, one of which was returned 70 yards for a touchdown. Philadelphia lost 24–14 to the Cardinals in St. Louis. But it was only a blip on the radar. They came back to Philadelphia the next week and defeated the Washington Redskins 24–14. They followed that up with a 31–16 victory over the New York Giants, although that win was a little shaky at first, with the Eagles down 16–3 at halftime.

Next the team came back home for a showdown with their divisional rivals, the Dallas Cowboys, with the first-place spot in the NFC East at stake. Dallas took a 7–0 lead when linebacker Mike Hegman recovered a Jaworski fumble in the end zone. But Jaworski redeemed himself, coming back to throw touchdown passes to Carmichael and Charlie Smith. The Eagles led 17–10, but the Cowboys were knocking on the door in the final seconds of the game with Dallas quarterback Danny White attempting to hit receiver Tony Hill in the end zone on fourth down. But Roynell Young broke up the pass to nail down the win for the Eagles.

After that, one victory followed another—a 17–14 win over the Chicago Bears, a 27–20 victory over the Seattle Seahawks, a 34–21 beating of the New Orleans Saints, and then a 24–0 shutout of the Redskins in Washington. Their next opponent would be the bad boys of the NFL, the Oakland Raiders, who came to town with their typical swagger. But the Eagles showed they were not intimidated, defeating the Raiders 10–7. It was a defensive victory—the Eagles pass rush sacked quarterback Jim Plunkett eight times.

The victory over the Raiders, along with a cross-country trip the next weekend, must have taken a lot out of the Eagles—they lost to the Chargers in San Diego 22–21 and had to battle back from a 19–0 third-quarter deficit to get

## TRIVIA

**What is the franchise record for attendance in a single season?**

*Answers to the trivia questions are on pages 160–161.*

even that close. The loss fell on the shoulders of kicker Tony Franklin, who missed field goals of 49, 36, and 56 yards.

The following week would deepen doubts about the team, as it lost for the first time at home to the Atlanta Falcons, the team that had beaten the Eagles in the wild-card game two years before, by a score of 20–17. Now they had dropped two straight and, with a record of 11–3,

*Ron Jaworski, shown here being chased by John Matuszak, was hounded all day by the Oakland Raiders defense in Super Bowl XV, as the Raiders intercepted three Jaworski passes in a 27–10 Oakland victory.* Photo courtesy of AP/Wide World Photos.

they were still in a battle with the Cowboys for the division title. They needed to keep up their earlier pace, and they did so with a 17–3 victory over the Cardinals.

They would meet the Cowboys again in their season finale, losing 35–27 and leaving the two teams tied, each with a 12–4 record. But the tiebreaker set forth by league rules was net points scored during the season, putting Philadelphia on top. One unfortunate side note from that Dallas game was that Carmichael failed to catch a pass, breaking his streak of catching a pass in 127 consecutive games.

Vermeil's team would be making their third straight playoff appearance, though their goals had now gone far beyond a mere post-season showing. Their championship dreams, however, were nearly destroyed by the Minnesota Vikings before a stunned crowd of 68,434 at Veterans Stadium. Down 14–0 in the second quarter, Jaworski hit Carmichael with a nine-yard touchdown pass to close the game to 14–7 at halftime. The Eagles tied it up when Montgomery scored on an eight-yard run on the team's first possession of the second half. The Vikings got back on top, 16–14, when they caught Jaworski in his own end zone for a two-point safety. But the Eagles kept things close, using the defense and special teams to create turnovers. The Vikings fumbled a punt, setting up Philadelphia for a Montgomery touchdown run late in the third quarter for a 21–16 Philadelphia lead. Minnesota fumbled the ball away in their next possession, and their final four possessions of the game ended with interceptions, for a total of eight turnovers in a 31–16 Eagles victory.

Appropriately enough, Philadelphia would play the Cowboys in the NFC championship game; winning the tie breaker against Dallas earlier had given the Eagles the home-field advantage for the game. Montgomery truly took the team on his shoulders in this contest, scoring the first touchdown on a 42-yard run and finishing with 196 yards on 22 carries for a 20–7 victory.

The Eagles were the NFC champions; more importantly, they were on their way to their first Super Bowl and their first chance at the NFL championship in 20 years. Best of all, there was no reason not to feel confident about their chances, since they were facing an AFC champion they had already beaten earlier in the season—the Oakland Raiders, who were their conference's wild-card team.

## All-1970s Team

| Position | Name |
|---|---|
| Coach | Dick Vermeil |
| *Offense* | |
| Wide Receiver | Harold Jackson |
| | Harold Carmichael |
| Tight End | Charle Young |
| Tackle | Stan Walters |
| | Jerry Sisemore |
| Guard | Wade Key |
| | Woody Peoples |
| Center | Guy Morriss |
| Quarterback | Ron Jaworski |
| Running Back | Wilbert Montgomery |
| Fullback | Mike Hogan |
| *Defense* | |
| End | Carl Hairston |
| | Claude Humphrey |
| Nose Tackle | Charlie Johnson |
| Linebacker | Bill Bergey |
| | Frank LeMaster |
| | John Bunting |
| Cornerback | Herman Edwards |
| | Joe Lavender |
| Safety | Bill Bradley |
| | Randy Logan |
| Kicker | Tom Dempsey |
| Kick Returner | Wilbert Montgomery |

The coverage leading up to Super Bowl XV in New Orleans was all about the partying Raiders, and how they were taking full advantage of the nightlife of Bourbon Street while Vermeil kept his own players on a tight leash. Unfortunately, Vermeil couldn't do the same with the Raiders' pass rush, led by John Matuszak, who forced Jaworski to rush his passes throughout the game. Three of those passes wound up in the hands of Raiders linebacker Rod Martin. On the other side of the ball, the powerful Eagles defense could not stop quarterback Jim Plunkett, who was named Super Bowl Most Valuable Player after throwing three touchdowns in a 27–10 Raiders victory. An eight-yard touchdown pass from Jaworski to Keith Krepfle and a Tony Franklin field goal were all the offense the Eagles could muster.

Looking back at the disappointing game, some Eagles believed they might have left their best game on the field two weeks earlier in the win over Dallas. "The NFC championship game was our Super Bowl," said Bergey, who retired after the season. "We had really set our sights on the Dallas Cowboys."

Still, it was a year worth savoring for Eagles fans. Jaworski threw for 27 touchdowns and 3,529 yards and was named NFL Player of the Year by the Maxwell Football Club and NFC Player of the Year by United Press International. Jaworski, Carmichael, safety Randy Logan, and defensive tackle Charlie Johnson were all named to the Pro Bowl. And the team as a whole set a franchise record with 14 victories, including playoff wins, in one season.

# Burnout

There was hope going into the 1981 season that the progress Dick Vermeil had made since his arrival could still result in a Super Bowl championship for the Eagles. Some hoped the experience of playing in the big game—despite losing—would better prepare them for the next time.

But there was no next time, at least not for this team.

They had lost team leader and defensive anchor Bill Bergey, who retired after the 1980 season. And the front office hardly had a banner year in the draft, selecting defensive end Leonard Mitchell out of Houston in the first round. He was a huge disappointment, and would later be switched to offensive tackle, where he did not distinguish himself either.

Still, in the first half of the season the team appeared to have picked up right where they left off, seeming well on their way to the big game. They won their opener against the New York Giants 24–10, then came home and defeated the New England Patriots 13–3. They had a short week preparing for game three, a Thursday night contest in Buffalo, but they showed no ill effects from the timing of the game, defeating the Bills 20–14 with Ron Jaworski completing 20 of 32 passes for 240 yards and two touchdowns while Wilbert Montgomery ran for 125 yards.

After defeating the Washington Redskins 36–13 at home to achieve a 4–0 record, week five would see the Eagles host the team, in a Monday night game, that had caused them so many problems over the past few years—the Atlanta Falcons. This time the Eagles would finally come away with a win, 16–13, but it was a tough one. Rookie fullback Hubie Oliver carried the ball 10 times and gained 68 yards, Tony Franklin kicked field goals of 34, 36, and 43 yards, and the defense intercepted Falcons quarterback Steve Bartkowski twice.

Philadelphia went to 6–0 with a 31–14 victory over the New Orleans Saints, then lost to the Vikings 35–23. That loss was followed by a 20–10 victory over Tampa Bay at home, and then a 17–14 loss to the Cowboys before a home crowd of 72,111. But two impressive wins—52–10 over the Cardinals in St. Louis and 38–13 over the Baltimore Colts at home—made it seem as if the Eagles were back on track to run through the rest of their schedule and meet the challenge of defending their NFC crown.

Then a 20–10 loss to the Giants sent the team into a tailspin. It was an unexpected defeat, as the Eagles had defeated the Giants 12 straight times before this game—but as Philadelphia would find out later, these were not the same doormat Giants they had played before.

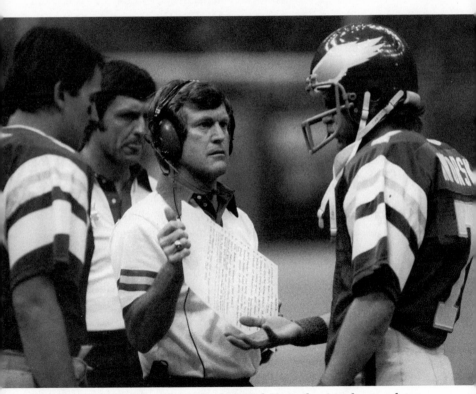

*After leading the Eagles to Super Bowl XV, Dick Vermeil resigned as coach two years later, citing "burnout." He ranks third among all-time Eagles coaches with 57 wins from 1976 to 1982.* Photo courtesy of AP/Wide World Photos.

That Eagles owner Leonard Tose once owned a trucking business that grossed more than $20 million a year? He was known for his extravagant ways, flying to Eagles games in a helicopter and serving filet mignon and shrimp cocktails to reporters who covered the team. But he was a compulsive gambler, and his addiction forced him to sell the franchise in 1985 for $65 million. By the end of his life he would lose everything. In 1996, on his 81st birthday, he was evicted from his seven-bedroom Villanova mansion after losing the house in a U.S. Marshal's sale. Three years later he told a congressional hearing on compulsive gambling that his losses totaled between $40 million and $50 million.

The Eagles next lost three straight on the road—13–10 to the Miami Dolphins, 15–13 to the Washington Redskins, and 21–10 to the Dallas Cowboys—before coming home and blasting the Cardinals 38–0 in the season's last game. Philadelphia finished with a 10–6 mark, still good enough to make the playoffs as a wild card; they would have to face the Giants at home in the wild-card playoff contest.

The Eagles entered the December 27 game with a weak hand—or in the case of Eagles kick returner Wally Henry, weak hands. Henry fumbled two returns—a punt that set up the first Giants score and the kickoff following the second touchdown. The Giants controlled the ball for much of the second half, thanks to 161 yards rushing by Rob Carpenter, and ended the Eagles' season far earlier than had been expected with a 27–21 defeat.

It was a hollow feeling for both the Eagles and their fans—it seemed to be such a waste of what had started out as an outstanding season. The defense had allowed the fewest yards (4,447) and points (221) in the league. Montgomery rushed for a career-high 1,402 yards and Harold Carmichael had his third 1,000-yard receiving year. But all they had to show for it was 10 wins and a playoff loss—pretty much the same place they had been back in 1978.

And then things got really bad.

Philadelphia faced the Washington Redskins in their 1982 season opener, a pivotal game that would send both franchises in different directions for years to come. The Eagles took a 10–0 lead in the first quarter. Then Washington kick returner Mike Nelms fumbled a kickoff, giving the Eagles the ball back on the Redskins' 18-yard line. But

Montgomery coughed the ball up on the 15-yard line and the Redskins recovered. Washington quarterback Joe Theismann drove the Redskins to two scores with a five-yard touchdown pass to Art Monk and an eight-yard touchdown reception by Charlie Brown. The Redskins had a 14–10 lead with less than a minute left in the first half, but Philadelphia added another 44-yard field goal by Franklin after Jaworski hit Carmichael on a 46-yard pass. The two teams battled back and forth; when the clock finally ran out in regulation, the score was tied 34–34. Washington got the ball in overtime and, after several Theismann to Monk connections, put kicker Mark Moseley in position to win the game, which he did with a 26-yard field goal for a 37–34 Redskins victory.

Years later, Redskins coach Joe Gibbs talked about the impact the game had on his team. "Philly had a heck of a football team," he said. "They had been to the playoffs the year before, and went to the Super Bowl two years before that. When we went up there to play them, I felt that was one of the key turning points in all of our games that we ever played with the Redskins. It was a tremendous victory that got us rolling."

It got the Eagles rolling in another direction. They managed to beat Cleveland in a close 24–21 game in week two. Then came the NFL strike and eight weeks without football. Some teams stayed together during the strike and were prepared when play resumed on November 21. The Eagles did not. They came back and lost four straight before beating Houston 35–14 at home followed by a 24–20 victory over the Cowboys in Dallas. It would be Vermeil's last win as coach of the Eagles. The team finished the season with a 26–24 loss to the Giants and a 3–6 record.

Citing burnout, an emotional Vermeil surprised everyone when he resigned at the end of the season. Luckily, the transition to a new coach would be relatively smooth because the new man—defensive coordinator Marion Campbell—was a familiar face who had the endorsement of the man he was succeeding. "When we went to the Super Bowl, I got the credit because I was head man. But we never would have gotten there without Marion and his staff," said Vermeil. Campbell was handed a setback when Montgomery suffered a knee injury that knocked him out for much of the season. But the team was helped by the arrival of a rookie who had an immediate impact—first-round choice Mike Quick, who would become one of the league's premier receivers.

The Good Guys

In 1984 the NFL created the Ed Block Courage Award—named for a beloved former Baltimore Colts trainer—to honor players who exemplified commitment to sportsmanship and courage. Tight end John Spagnola was the first winner for the Eagles. Other Eagles winners were:

Ron Jaworski
Jody Schulz
Gerry Feehery
Wes Hopkins
Mike Quick
Ron Solt
David Alexander
Jerome Brown
Andre Waters
Fred Barnett
Charlie Garner
Kevin Turner
Rhett Hall
Bobby Taylor
Mike Mamula
Duce Staley and Tommy Brasher
    (cowinners in 2001)
Shawn Barber
Correll Buckhalter and Derrick Burgess
    (cowinners in 2004)
Chad Lewis

Campbell seemed like the right man for the job when Philadelphia opened the 1983 season with a 22–17 win over the 49ers in San Francisco. They then won three of their next five games, including an impressive 17–13 win over the Giants in New York in which Jaworski threw two touchdown passes to Quick, who caught six passes that day for 72 yards. But the Eagles were manhandled 37–7 the following week by the Cowboys in a game that was supposed to be played in

Philadelphia but was moved to Dallas because the Phillies were hosting the Baltimore Orioles in the World Series. It was the franchise's worst defeat in eight years. The Eagles opened the game with an 83-yard touchdown pass from Jaworski to Quick. They did nothing after that, and the same could be said for the rest of the season. They lost eight of their last nine games and finished the year with a 5–11 record. Jaworski had a good year, with 20 touchdown passes and 18 interceptions, throwing for 3,315 yards, and Quick was named All-Pro, leading the league with 1,409 yards on 69 catches and 13 touchdowns. But without Montgomery the Eagles had no running game.

The 1984 season went in the opposite direction. After a 1–4 start, the Eagles posted a 5–5–1 record in their final 11 games. The defense set a club record with 60 quarterback sacks. Montgomery established franchise records in rushing with 6,538 yards as well as in attempts with 1,465, surpassing the marks set by Steve Van Buren. Kicker Paul McFadden set an Eagles rookie scoring record with 116 points and was named NFC Rookie of the Year. But Jaworski suffered a broken leg in week 13 against St. Louis, ending his streak of 116 consecutive starts.

A huge change for the franchise took place in March 1985 when Tose, suffering from a series of gambling losses that would eventually leave him broke, sold the team to Florida automobile dealers Norman Braman and Ed Leibowitz for $65 million. Braman put general manager Harry Gamble in charge of the team as vice president and general manager. In another big change for the team, Montgomery did not report to training camp and was traded to the Detroit Lions for linebacker Garry Cobb before the season began.

As the 1985 season got under way it became clear that the era of Vermeil, carried over by his defensive coach Campbell, was over. The Eagles lost four of their first five games and finished with a 7–9 record. Campbell was fired on December 16 and one of his assistants, Fred Bruney, took over as interim coach for the final game against Minnesota—a 37–35 win.

A new era was about to begin, and it would be like nothing Eagles fans had ever seen before. They would soon have a new "Buddy," who would change everything.

# "Bud-dee, Bud-dee"

When the Chicago Bears won the 1986 Super Bowl, the players carried not one but two coaches on their shoulders to celebrate—head coach Mike Ditka and defensive coordinator Buddy Ryan.

It was the first time in the history of the game that an assistant coach got such attention, but Ryan was an assistant in name only. In his mind he was the boss, and his players loved him for the courage of his convictions—even if it meant feuding with Ditka, another well-known tough guy who came to be known as "Da Coach." Ryan was fearless, both on and off the field. He filled up reporters' notebooks with uncoachlike quotes, brashly touting his own abilities and those of his team. Finally, on January 29, 1986, Ryan had a title to go along with his ego when he was hired as the head coach of the Philadelphia Eagles.

He wouldn't have too much to brag about in his first season, though; the Eagles finished with a 5–10–1 record, good for only fourth place in the NFC East. Still, he was accomplishing what he set out to do when he took over—cleaning out the players who weren't with the program and bringing in "Buddy" guys like rookies Seth Joyner and Keith Byars. He also began starting some of the younger players he had inherited, including an immensely talented quarterback out of the University of Nevada–Las Vegas named Randall Cunningham. The defense, led by defensive end Reggie White—one of the club's rewards in the United States Football League dispersal draft—increasingly began to resemble Buddy's "46 Defense" Bears.

"Any Eagles fan will tell you the greatest thing Buddy brought to the table was the 46 defensive scheme, which was perfect for our personnel—

with Seth [Joyner], and Andre [Waters]—because we would just attack and get after the quarterback," said linebacker Mike Reichenbach. "That defense was designed solely to kill the quarterback."

The Eagles were the ones taking a beating initially, as Ryan lost his debut to the division rival Redskins 41–14 in Washington. It wasn't until week four that the new coach would finally earn a victory, a 34–20 win over the Los Angeles Rams at home. The defense held the league's top rusher, Eric Dickerson, to only 58 yards rushing, while Byars rushed for 78 yards on 17 carries and Ron Jaworski completed 17 of 27 passes for 213 yards and three touchdowns.

The Eagles would win only four more games that year. Jaworski injured a tendon in his throwing hand during week 10 and was gone for the season, putting the offense in the hands—and on the feet—of Cunningham. Ryan was impressed enough with the young quarterback

*Under head coach Buddy Ryan, the Eagles put together some stellar playoff seasons but never a return to the Super Bowl.*

that in March 1987 the team put Jaworski on waivers after the club decided not to guarantee his contract.

Unfortunately for Philadelphia, the 1987 season would turn out to be a repeat of 1982. The Eagles split the first two games of the season, and then the players went on strike. After a week of canceled games, the league continued with the schedule using replacement players. Just as in 1982, the Redskins benefited from the strike, coming up with a strong replacement team that went 3–0, while the Eagles replacement players were winless in three games. When the starters returned, the team had a 1–4 record.

After the strike ended, the team won three straight and finished 7–8 for the season, 7–5 in games with the regular players. They finished the season with a 17–7 victory over the Buffalo Bills at home, an impressive defensive effort that held Jim Kelly and the powerful Bills offense to only 191 total yards. Mike Quick earned his fifth consecutive trip to the Pro Bowl, with 46 catches for 790 yards and 11 touchdowns. Cunningham emerged as an NFL star, throwing 23 touchdowns and gaining 505 yards on the ground, becoming the first quarterback to lead his team in rushing since the Bears' Bobby Douglass in 1971. White had 21 quarterback sacks, setting an NFC record, and was named NFL Defensive Player of the Year. The defense was made even stronger by the addition of outstanding rookie defensive tackle Jerome Brown, who joined Clyde Simmons and Mike Pitts to form the league's premier defensive line.

The parts were in place for an outstanding 1988 season, and all signs pointed to such a year in the season debut, a 41–14 beating of the Tampa Bay Buccaneers. But the bottom seemed to fall out in week two with a 28–24 loss to the Cincinnati Bengals, followed by two straight losses on the road to the Washington Redskins and the Minnesota Vikings. Ryan's team righted itself briefly with two wins at the Vet against the Houston Oilers and the New York Giants. It then lost to Cleveland, beat Dallas by only one point (24–23), and was beaten 27–24 by the Atlanta Falcons.

The Eagles were 4–5 and mired in mediocrity when a 30–24 victory over the Los Angeles Rams before 65,624 hometown fans put the train back on the tracks. Cunningham had an outstanding game, completing 22 of 39 passes for 323 yards and running for 53 yards. The defense secured the win with the Rams marching down the field in the closing minutes when White sacked Los Angeles quarterback Jim Everett for a 10-yard loss, followed by an interception two plays later by William Frizzell.

The Eagles went on to win five of their final six games for a 10–6 record—the franchise's first winning record in seven years and good enough for the NFC East division title. However they didn't secure their playoff spot until a few minutes after their 23–7 win over the Cowboys at Dallas in the final game of the season. Shortly after the Eagles game ended, New York Jets quarterback Ken O'Brien hit Al Toon with a game-winning touchdown pass to defeat the New York Giants, giving Philadelphia the top division spot.

The Eagles would go to Chicago to face the Bears in the first round of the playoffs for a much-anticipated showdown between Ryan and Ditka. But the game, which came to be known as the "Fog Bowl," was notable more for the strange weather than for anything that happened on the field. Despite the sunshine at the start of the game at Soldier Field, a thick fog soon rolled off Lake Michigan and engulfed the stadium, severely limiting visibility on the field. The Bears won 20–12.

Cunningham had a stellar year, throwing for 3,808 yards and 24 touchdowns. He also led the team in rushing for the second consecutive season, gaining 624 yards. He won the Bert Bell Award from the Maxwell Football Club, an honor awarded to the NFL's top player. White led the league in sacks for the second straight season. Tight end Keith Jackson set a club record with 81 catches and was named NFL Rookie of the Year by *The Sporting News*. Cunningham, White, and Jackson were all named to the Pro Bowl, where Cunningham was also named MVP, the second such honor for an Eagles player in three years.

The playoff loss to the Bears left a bitter taste in the mouths of this Eagles squad, and they played like a team on a mission as the 1989 season got underway. They opened with a 31–7 win over the Seattle Seahawks at home, then faced the division rival Redskins in Washington in week two. The game was on its way into the loss column with Washington leading by 20 points before the end of the first half. The Eagles battled back but were losing 37–35 with 1:16 left in

## TRIVIA

**Which player threw for 338 yards in a 41–22 loss to the Cowboys in 1987?**

*Answers to the trivia questions are on pages 160–161.*

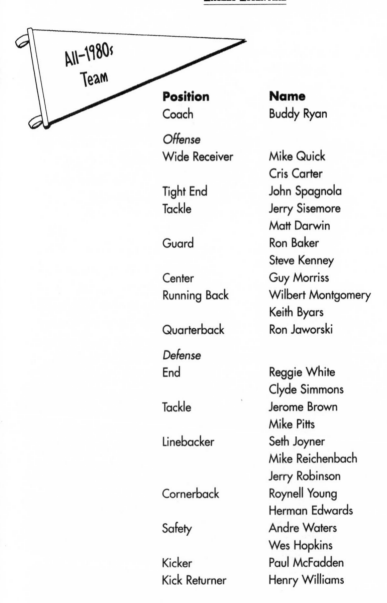

**All-1980s Team**

| Position | Name |
| --- | --- |
| Coach | Buddy Ryan |
| *Offense* | |
| Wide Receiver | Mike Quick |
| | Cris Carter |
| Tight End | John Spagnola |
| Tackle | Jerry Sisemore |
| | Matt Darwin |
| Guard | Ron Baker |
| | Steve Kenney |
| Center | Guy Morriss |
| Running Back | Wilbert Montgomery |
| | Keith Byars |
| Quarterback | Ron Jaworski |
| *Defense* | |
| End | Reggie White |
| | Clyde Simmons |
| Tackle | Jerome Brown |
| | Mike Pitts |
| Linebacker | Seth Joyner |
| | Mike Reichenbach |
| | Jerry Robinson |
| Cornerback | Roynell Young |
| | Herman Edwards |
| Safety | Andre Waters |
| | Wes Hopkins |
| Kicker | Paul McFadden |
| Kick Returner | Henry Williams |

the game. Washington had possession of the ball on Philadelphia's 22-yard line when running back Gerald Riggs fumbled and Eagles linebacker Al Harris picked it up. Just as Harris was about to be tackled, Eagles safety Wes Hopkins took the ball out of his hands and ran 77 yards to the Washington 4-yard line before being tackled by Redskins receiver

Ricky Sanders. Cunningham then found Jackson in the end zone for a touchdown and a 42–37 victory. The Eagles players gathered along the sidelines at RFK Stadium and chanted, "Bud-dee! Bud-dee! Bud-dee!" They were mocking the Redskins fans, who had started the "Bud-dee!" chant back in the first quarter, when Washington was ahead 20–0.

Philadelphia would go on to finish with an 11–5 record, only good enough for second place in the NFC East. The Eagles hosted the Los Angeles Rams in the wild-card playoff game, losing 21–7 in a rainy, forgettable contest in which Philadelphia fell behind 21–0 and scored only in the fourth quarter on a one-yard run by Anthony Toney.

The Eagles defense had a quality year, leading the league in takeaways, with 56, and interceptions, with 30, and set a team record with 62 sacks. But they were one-and-done in the playoffs for the second straight season, prompting some grumbling that the offense would need improvement before the team could hope to go any further in the postseason. In response Ryan hired Rich Kotite as offensive coordinator in the hopes of improving the Eagles' production. On paper the move paid dividends. At the end of the season the offense, which had no rushing offense during the two previous years, led the league in rushing, with 2,556 yards, and in time of possession, averaging 33:19 per game. They also led the NFC in scoring, with 396 points, and in touchdown passes, with 34. Meanwhile the defense led the league in rushing defense, making the Eagles the first team to lead the league in both offensive rushing and rushing defense since the Super Bowl XX–champion Bears coached by Ditka (and Ryan, of course).

Still, the Eagles would not have a Super Bowl to show for their efforts. They finished 10–6, again only good enough for a wild-card playoff slot, and then, for the third straight season, lost in the playoffs in the first round, this time going down at the hands of the Washington Redskins 20–6. Cunningham had a remarkable season, with 30 touchdown passes and 942 yards rushing. Byars was a pass-catching machine coming out of the backfield, tying a team record with 81 catches. He also threw four touchdown passes. Rookie wide receivers Fred Barnett and Calvin Williams combined for 17 touchdown catches.

Despite these strong performances, with three early playoff exits, Ryan had worn out his welcome. He was fired by Norman Braman in January.

# Head Coach Changes: Ryan to Kotite

It turns out that when Buddy Ryan hired Rich Kotite to be his offensive coordinator in 1990, he actually hired his own replacement. On January 8, 1991—the same day that owner Norman Braman decided to fire Ryan—Braman announced his decision to promote Kotite to head coach.

He could not have been more different than the blustery, colorful man he was replacing. Where Ryan was impossible to ignore in nearly any situation, Kotite was impossible to notice. He had a bland personality and offered none of the journalist-pleasing quotes for which Ryan was so well known. And in Philadelphia—where a coach has to connect with the fans to be successful—Kotite actually turned fans off. He benefited, however, from the work Ryan had done in his first two seasons—the defense put together by the previous coach reached its zenith in 1991. Kotite put the defense in the hands of another legendary defensive coordinator, Bud Carson.

The defense finished the season ranked first in the NFL in yards allowed overall, versus both the run and the pass, becoming only the fifth club in league history and the first since 1975 to do so. The defense also led the league in sacks and fumble recoveries and tied for the league lead in takeaways. Five Eagles players—defensive ends Reggie White and Clyde Simmons, defensive tackle Jerome Brown, cornerback Eric Allen, and linebacker Seth Joyner—were named to the Pro Bowl, the first time in NFL history that three defensive linemen from the same team were named to that contest. White led the league with 15 sacks and was named NFL Defensive Player of the Year by *Pro Football Weekly*.

They would need all that defensive ability in the season to come. In the opener at Green Bay the Eagles defeated the Packers 20–3 but lost their offensive star, quarterback Randall Cunningham, when he suffered torn ligaments in his left knee, an injury that would end his season. The team then turned to one of Ryan's boys, former Bears quarterback Jim McMahon, who was now a backup to Cunningham. The offense struggled in the home opener against the Phoenix Cardinals with five fumbles and a McMahon interception.

In week three the offense did what they needed to do, protecting the ball and stopping turnovers, against a young but inexperienced Dallas Cowboys team, coming away with a 24–0 shutout victory. The defense allowed only 90 yards of total offense and sacked Dallas quarterback Troy Aikman 11 times. McMahon passed for 207 yards, just enough to win the game.

McMahon would be pummeled two weeks later in a 23–0 defeat by the Redskins, injuring his knee in the process. Kotite switched back and forth for the next four weeks between Pat Ryan, Brad Goebel, and Jeff Kemp at quarterback, with little success—the Eagles lost four straight and were now 3–5 halfway through the season. McMahon was healthy and ready to play by week nine, however, and James Joseph and the running game began to produce as the Eagles beat the New York Giants 30–7. The offense gained 137 yards rushing and McMahon completed 16 of 26 passes for 229 yards, with Keith Jackson catching four of those passes for 88 yards of his own.

Next the team traveled to Cleveland to play the Browns in what would be one of the most memorable Eagles games in recent memory. After trailing the Browns 23–0, Philadelphia came back to win the game 32–30. Despite knee and elbow injuries, McMahon put on a courageous show, completing 26 of 43 passes for 341 yards and three touchdowns including an 18-yarder to Jackson, a 70-yard play to Fred Barnett, and a five-yard scoring pass to Calvin Williams. It was a remarkable comeback

**DID YOU KNOW . . .** That from 1985 to 2000, Reggie White recorded 198 sacks for the Eagles and the Green Bay Packers, an NFL record until Bruce Smith extended his career specifically to break the record in 2003? White had 23.5 sacks while playing 34 games with the Memphis Showboats in the United States Football League before he arrived in Philadelphia, giving him a career total of 221.5 sacks.

that propelled the Eagles to a strong finish and a winning season. The Eagles won five of their next six games for a 10–6 record, good for only third in the NFC East and not good enough to make the playoffs.

In 1992, with Cunningham once again healthy and the acquisition of running back Herschel Walker, who would rush for 1,070 yards, the Eagles built on what they had done the previous year. This time they made the playoffs, finishing with an 11–5 record. But despite its success, a dark cloud hung over the franchise. All-Pro defensive tackle Jerome Brown was killed in an automobile accident on June 25 in his hometown of Brooksville, Florida. The tragedy overshadowed the promise of the upcoming season.

Week 15 would bring 65,841 fans to Veterans Stadium to witness a key 17–13 victory over division rivals and defending champions Washington, D.C. The Redskins had defeated Philadelphia 16–12 earlier in the season and appeared ready to snatch this game away as well when, with only seconds left and the Redskins on the Eagles' 5-yard line, Simmons got his hand on a Mark Rypien pass. Allen then knocked the ball down to preserve the win, which assured the Eagles of a wild-card playoff appearance.

Kotite distanced himself from Ryan in one important way in 1992—his team won a playoff game—a 36–20 win over the Saints in New Orleans. It was the first postseason victory for the Eagles since 1980. Running back Heath Sherman gained 105 yards on 21 carries, while Cunningham completed 19 of 35 passes for 219 yards. Saints quarterback Bobby Hebert was intercepted twice, once by Eric Allen and another time by Seth Joyner. But the Eagles' season ended the following week when the Cowboys easily disposed of them 34–10 in Dallas.

The 1993 season was a brave new world in the NFL—the beginning of legitimate free agency. The Eagles were hit where it hurts when White, a true team leader, left to sign with the Green Bay Packers, where he would help his new teammates win a Super Bowl championship. Defensive tackles Mike Golic and Mike Pitts also left, as did Keith Byars, McMahon, and six other players. Quarterback Bubby Brister, defensive end Tim Harris, and defensive tackle Keith Millard were among the new arrivals.

At the start of the season the team seemed to have absorbed the personnel losses without too much trouble, opening with a 23–17 victory

*Running back Herschel Walker had a brief stay with the Eagles, from 1992 to 1994, but he is in the franchise record books for the longest run from scrimmage, gaining 91 yards on a play against the Falcons in 1994.*

By the
NUMBERS

**7**—The number of consecutive Pro Bowls Reggie White appeared in, a franchise record. The Pro Bowl was White's game: he was also named its Most Valuable Player in 1987.

over Phoenix and going on to win their next three, including a 20–17 triumph over the Packers and White, their former teammate. But in their 35–30 win over the New York Jets, Cunningham suffered a broken leg, and wide receiver Fred Barnett tore knee ligaments. Relying on Bubby Brister at quarterback, the Eagles lost eight of their next nine games before managing to win their last three games—including a 37–34 overtime victory in the season finale against the 49ers in San Francisco—finishing with an 8–8 record.

The franchise was turned over to a new owner once more when Braman announced on April 6 that he had sold the team to Jeffrey Lurie, a Boston native and president of a film production company. Lurie officially took over the franchise on May 17, arriving just in time to preside over the fall of the club. Joyner and Clyde Simmons left for free agency in 1994, joining former coach Buddy Ryan, who had been hired to run the Arizona Cardinals. Cunningham was not the same quarterback after his injuries the previous season, and his self-centered personality had become a locker-room problem. Meanwhile Walker could not duplicate his 1,000-yard season from the year before.

After starting 7–2, the Eagles lost their final seven games to earn a 7–9 record, and Kotite lost his job.

# A Milestone on the Sidelines

Eagles owner Jeff Lurie made a historic hire in 1995 when he named San Francisco 49ers defensive coordinator Ray Rhodes as Philadelphia's new head coach—the first black head coach in the franchise's history and only the third in the league.

However Rhodes wasn't Lurie's first choice. The Eagles owner had first wanted to lure Dick Vermeil back to the team, and he had also made overtures to Jimmy Johnson. But a call from Bill Walsh—the offensive coaching genius who led the San Francisco 49ers to three Super Bowl championships in the 1980s—recommending Rhodes helped move the defensive guru to the front of the line.

Initially, it seemed as if Lurie and Eagles general manager Joe Bannon had made a mistake. The Eagles lost their home opener 21–6 to Tampa Bay, but bounced back to defeat the Cardinals in Arizona 31–19. They then lost two straight, first a 27–21 loss to the San Diego Chargers and then an embarrassing 48–17 beating at the hands of the Raiders in Oakland.

But, as is often the case with a new head coach, it would just take some time for the players to adjust to a new system and an unfamiliar way of doing things. Given Rhodes's forceful personality, coming on the heels of the laid-back Kotite, Eagles players certainly had some adjusting to do. One who didn't adapt well to the change was Randall Cunningham, who was benched in favor of Rodney Peete. Cunningham had become a destabilizing presence on the team with his erratic personality, while Peete was seen as a calming influence.

After beating the Saints on the road 15–10, the Eagles came home for an October 8 showdown against their division rival Washington Redskins in a game that would set the tone for the rest of the team's season. Philadelphia took a 7–0 lead in the first quarter when Charlie Garner ran 55

# TRIVIA

**Who were the brothers who were both quarterbacks and who were on the Eagles' roster at the same time?**

*Answers to the trivia questions are on pages 160–161.*

yards for a touchdown. Washington kicker Eddie Murray nailed a 36-yard field goal to cut the Eagles' lead to 7–3; then Brian Mitchell returned a punt 59 yards for a 10–7 Redskins' margin. Eagles kicker Gary Anderson tied it late in the first quarter with a 40-yard field goal.

Philadelphia took a 24–17 lead into the locker room at halftime, but Redskins quarterback Gus Frerotte ran it over on a bootleg in the third quarter to tie the game 24–24. The Eagles jumped forward again later on in the quarter when Garner scored on a 17-yard touchdown run and Anderson hit a 43-yard field goal for a 34–24 Eagles lead. But Washington came back once again on a 12-yard touchdown pass from Frerotte to Henry Ellard and a 46-yard Murray field goal, and the score was 34–34 when time ran out. After the Eagles forced the Redskins to punt on the first possession of the overtime, Philadelphia moved down the field methodically, handing the ball to both Garner and Ricky Watters. Then Peete found Fred Barnett on a 16-yard pass play, and after several Watters runs, Anderson hit a 35-yard game-winning field goal for a 37–34 victory. The game was a confidence booster that seemed to bond Rhodes and his players.

The Eagles ended the season as one of the league's hottest teams, winning nine of their final 12 games and finishing with a 10–6 record, winding up in second place in the NFC East. They then went on to defeat the Detroit Lions 58–37 in the wild-card game, scoring 31 points in the second quarter alone before a crowd of 66,099 at the Vet. They then lost 30–11 to the Cowboys in Dallas in the divisional playoff contest.

Watters, who had signed as a free agent, rushed for 1,273 yards for the season. Rhodes, meanwhile, was named NFL Coach of the Year. "I'm

## By the NUMBERS

**9-9-96**—The Eagles' offensive line has protected their quarterbacks well for the past 10 years, at least deep in their own territory. The last time a Philadelphia quarterback was tackled for a safety was on September 9, 1996, in a 39–13 loss to the Packers in Green Bay. Who were the Packers tacklers that day? Santana Dotson and a familiar face—Reggie White.

*When Ray Rhodes was hired in 1995, he was the first black head coach in Eagles history and only the third in the history of the league, but he was fired after four seasons and a 30–36–1 record.* Photo courtesy of AP/Wide World Photos.

127

not a guy who's big on personal achievements," he told reporters. "Anybody who knows me knows that. Really, this award is a reflection on this organization for making the commitment to get this thing pointed in the right direction."

It sure seemed as if the organization was moving in the right direction in 1996, when the Eagles opened the season with a 17–14 victory over the Redskins in Washington; the offense put up 310 yards in the first half, compared to 77 for the Redskins, even though those numbers didn't add up to a lot of points. Defensive end Mike Mamula harassed Redskins quarterback Frerotte all afternoon.

The squad lost 39–13 to Green Bay the following week, but won six of their next seven games and finished the season once again with a 10–6 record. Given their playoff experience, it seemed as if Philadelphia might be able to proceed further in the playoffs. But they were easily dispatched by the San Francisco 49ers in the wild-card game, losing 14–0. Philadelphia outgained the 49ers, but they couldn't deal with the San Francisco elements—rain and 51-mile-per-hour winds. Steve Young scored on a nine-yard run, following that with a three-yard touchdown pass to Jerry Rice.

It was an inconsistent year for the Eagles offense. Ty Detmer, who took over for Peete during the season, was hardly a playoff-caliber quarterback. There were bright spots in the form of Irving Fryar, who caught 88 passes for 1,195 yards and 11 touchdowns, and Ricky Watters, who rushed for 1,411 yards. Both made the Pro Bowl, as did defensive end William Fuller and linebacker William Thomas.

In 1997 Rhodes was still unable to straighten out his team's offensive woes; the team struggled with quarterbacks Ty Detmer and Bobby Hoying and dropped to a 6–9–1 record, finishing the season with three straight losses against the Giants (31–21), the Falcons (20–17), and finally the Redskins (35–32).

With the departure of Ricky Watters, the entire offense collapsed in 1998, scoring only 161 points over 16 games, and the Eagles dropped to 3–13, the franchise's worst record since 1972. Still, there were a couple of noteworthy

**TRIVIA**

**Before purchasing the Eagles from Norman Braman in 1994, Jeff Lurie was involved in another high-profile business. What was it?**

*Answers to the trivia questions are on pages 160–161.*

accomplishments. Second-year back Duce Staley emerged as an offensive star, leading the Eagles in rushing (1,065 yards), receptions (57), and total yards from scrimmage (1,497) to become the first Eagles draft pick to top the 1,000-yard rushing plateau since Wilbert Montgomery in 1981. On defense the Eagles found a leader in defensive end Hugh Douglas, a trade from the New York Jets who led the Eagles and finished seventh in the NFL with a career-high 12.5 sacks, including a club-tying record of 4.5 sacks in a 13–10 loss to San Diego.

Rhodes was fired, having called for his own firing when the season ended. "When you don't win, changes have to be made. This is part of the business," Rhodes said at a news conference with Lurie. Replacement candidates discussed in the media included well-known names like Wisconsin coach Barry Alvarez and former Carolina Panthers coach Dom Capers, who had been fired from his own position. But Lurie would call on a little-known offensive coach with a championship pedigree to bring the franchise into the 21st century.

# A Championship Pedigree

The Eagles didn't go to the college ranks for their next coach, as they had for Dick Vermeil. And they didn't go for a flamboyant, high-profile candidate, as they had with Buddy Ryan. They didn't even go the comfortable route, promoting someone from within the staff.

The Eagles went the inside NFL route and hired an unknown assistant with the best résumé in the league—a candidate with great "bloodlines," so to speak. Packers assistant coach Andy Reid had spent seven seasons under Mike Holmgren with Green Bay, during which time the Packers went to the playoffs six times and won a Super Bowl championship. "Everyone who works with him and plays for him knows exactly where he is coming from," said Eagles team president Joe Banner. "We wanted someone with a strong set of convictions and who wasn't going to be affected by ups and downs and public pressure."

They got their man when they hired Reid on January 11, 1999, but it was not the only man they got. Three months later the Eagles selected Syracuse quarterback Donovan McNabb with the second pick in the draft—despite the howls of protest from Eagles fans who booed the selection, demanding instead that the team take Heisman Trophy–winner Ricky Williams.

Reid and McNabb would prove the critics wrong. Reid made his debut as the Eagles coach at home in a tough 25–24 loss to the Arizona Cardinals. Going with the more experienced Doug Pederson at quarterback, Philadelphia lost three more before Reid finally got his first win as an NFL head coach, a 13–10 victory on October 10 over the Dallas Cowboys at the Vet. They won the following week against the Bears in Chicago but then went on a three-game losing streak. With the team holding a 2–7 record, the demanding Philadelphia fans were grumbling, and it wouldn't get much better when Reid opted to start McNabb.

But this was indeed a coach who seemed to be immune to the enormous public pressures that come with coaching in Philadelphia. He still had the same confidence in McNabb that he had had when he drafted the young quarterback out of Syracuse. It was a winning debut, as McNabb led the Eagles to a 35–28 win over the Washington Redskins before 66,591 spectators at Veterans Stadium. He would start six of the team's last seven games in 1999, and the Eagles won three of those last seven, a 35–28 win over Washington, a 24–9 win over New England, and a 38–31 victory over St. Louis—to wrap up the year and finish the season with a 5–11 mark.

There were signs that the team was about to play far better than its record might have predicted. Running back Duce Staley rushed for 1,273 yards in 1999, his second 1,000-yard season. McNabb threw for 948 yards and eight touchdowns in six starts and rushed for 313 yards. New defensive coordinator Jim Johnson was putting together a tough unit; his squad led the league with 46 takeaways, including 28 interceptions, five of which were returned for touchdowns, a team record. Safety Brian Dawkins and cornerback Troy Vincent earned their first Pro Bowl selections, and Vincent's seven interceptions tied for the league lead.

The franchise was on the rise, but no one could have seen how quickly it would improve when the 2000 season began. Kicker David Akers executed a perfect onside kick in the season opener in Dallas, which set the stage for the Eagles' 41–14 opening win over the Cowboys. After Staley went down for the season with a foot injury in game five, McNabb took over the offense, accounting for nearly 75 percent of the team's total net yards. He completed 330 passes out of 569 attempts for 3,365 yards and 21 touchdowns. He also rushed for

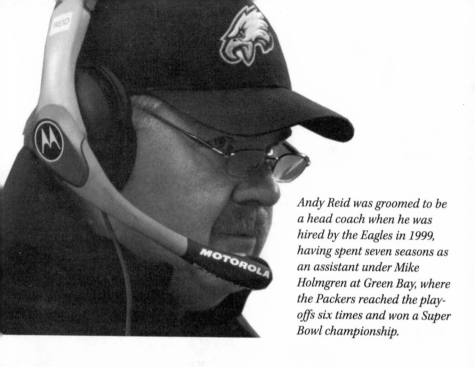

*Andy Reid was groomed to be a head coach when he was hired by the Eagles in 1999, having spent seven seasons as an assistant under Mike Holmgren at Green Bay, where the Packers reached the play-offs six times and won a Super Bowl championship.*

629 yards, averaging 7.3 yards per carry, and scored six touchdowns on the ground. The team's performance was good enough to earn the top wild-card spot in the NFC.

In the playoffs the Eagles overwhelmed Tampa Bay 21–3 before losing to the eventual NFC champion New York Giants in the divisional playoffs. Reid had engineered the greatest turnaround in Eagles history—the team finished with an 11–5 record, and Reid was named NFL Coach of the Year. McNabb finished second behind Rams running back Marshall Faulk in the voting for Associated Press Most Valuable Player. Tight end Chad Lewis led all NFC tight ends in receptions with 69 and earned his first trip to the Pro Bowl, joining McNabb, Vincent, linebacker Jeremiah Trotter, and defensive end Hugh Douglas.

The rise to the top continued in 2001. With a 2–2 record going into a *Monday Night Football* contest against New York at Giants Stadium, the Eagles won a hard-fought 10–9 game and then won eight of their next 11, including a dramatic 24–21 victory over the Giants once again, this time at home. At the end of the season the Eagles had captured their first NFC Eastern Division championship since 1988 and their first appearance in the NFC title game since 1980. They treated Eagles fans to an explosive home playoff victory when they beat Tampa Bay 31–9. Philadelphia moved a step closer to reaching the Super Bowl for the first time in 21 years when they beat the Bears in Chicago in the NFC divisional playoff. But they came up short against the high-powered St. Louis Rams offense in the NFC championship game, falling 29–24.

Eagles fans still came away feeling pretty good about their team and its future, as if somehow they knew that a magical season was ahead of them in 2002—the 32nd and final season at Veterans Stadium, as the franchise was about to move next door to the new $500-million Lincoln Financial Field the next year. They lost the opener in Tennessee to the Titans, 27–24. But they won six of their next eight games and appeared to be coasting to a championship run until disaster struck—McNabb broke his ankle on November 17 against the Cardinals in Arizona. Despite the injury, McNabb turned in one of the gutsiest performances in franchise history when he played nearly the entire game with the injury and led Philadelphia to a 38–14 win over Arizona, completing 20 out of 25 passes for 255 yards and four touchdowns. After that he was sidelined for the rest of the season in an attempt to heal before the playoffs, putting the season in the hands of his backup, A.J. Feeley. Feeley handled the job better than fans could have hoped for, throwing for 1,011 yards and six touchdowns while leading the team to five out of six wins to close out the regular season with a 12–4 record.

The Eagles finished first in the NFC East, receiving a first-round bye, and had home-field advantage in the two final conference playoff games. The team sent a record 10 players to the Pro Bowl. Staley rushed for 1,029 yards, and versatile rookie running back Brian Westbrook, out of Villanova, began to emerge as a future star. Akers set a franchise record with 133 points.

The Eagles had every reason to believe that this was their season. They beat Atlanta 20–6 in the divisional playoff and, in the final game at the Vet, faced the Tampa Bay Buccaneers in the NFC championship game. After beating the Falcons, McNabb put the team's expectations on the record. "We are excited, but yet we have another game left," he told reporters. "It is unfinished business. We set goals in the off-season of making it to San Diego [the site of the Super Bowl]. This is another opportunity for us to take a step forward."

Turns out they were standing in the same place after the NFC championship game—one step away from the Super Bowl. The Bucs trounced the Eagles 27–10, an unfortunate outcome for the team's final appearance at the Vet. It was particularly disappointing given the way the game opened—with a 70-yard kickoff return by Brian Mitchell. But the Bucs defense, led by Warren Sapp and Derrick Brooks, stifled the Eagles offense, shutting them out in the second half despite a strong performance from McNabb, who completed 26 of 49 passes for 243 yards in only his second game back from his broken ankle.

"They were the better team," Reid told reporters. "They got after us. We didn't answer the bell on a few things. It's very disappointing. You come this far, 20-some odd weeks of football. You put yourself in position to strike for the Super Bowl, and you lose."

Unfortunately, it was becoming an all-too-familiar position. The Eagles might have thought their new stadium, Lincoln Financial Field, was cursed after they lost their first two games of the 2003 season there—an embarrassing 17–0 loss in a rematch with the Bucs, who had gone on to defeat Oakland in the Super Bowl the previous season, and a 31–10 defeat at the hands of the New England Patriots. They struggled with injuries throughout the season, losing safety Dawkins and corner-back Bobby Taylor for much of the year with foot injuries. But after a 2–3 start, the Eagles rattled off nine straight wins, tying a team record set in 1960. That winning streak was propelled by a remarkable October 19 victory over the Giants on the road. With the Eagles trailing 10–7 with 1:34 remaining and no timeouts, Westbrook fielded a bouncing punt and ran 84 yards for the game-winning touchdown.

After suffering through a nagging thumb injury in his throwing hand, McNabb won NFC offensive player of the month honors in November, leading Philadelphia to a 5–0 month. With a second-straight 12–4 record, first place in the NFC East again, and home-field advantage once more in the playoffs, the Eagles had earned a third NFC championship appearance and one more chance to punch a ticket to the Super Bowl.

Just as in the previous two years, after reaching the title game the Eagles lost yet again, this time 14–3 to the Carolina Panthers. Eagles fans had gone through three years of what was perhaps the most painful 35–13 record any team ever had. The team's inability to get to the Super Bowl had now become a source of embarrassment. Desperate measures were needed. Desperate measures were pursued, and desperate measures would indeed be taken.

*When coach Andy Reid picked Syracuse's Donovan McNabb as the Eagles' number-one pick in 1999, Reid said he felt that McNabb was best suited to handle the pressure of playing in Philadelphia.*

All-1990s
Team

| Position | Name |
|----------|------|
| Coach | Rich Kotite |
| *Offense* | |
| Wide receiver | Fred Barnett |
| | Irving Fryar |
| Tight end | Keith Jackson |
| Tackle | Antone Davis |
| | Tra Thomas |
| Guard | Jermane Mayberry |
| | Mike Schad |
| Center | Steve Everitt |
| Running back | Duce Staley |
| | Herschel Walker |
| Quarterback | Randall Cunningham |
| *Defense* | |
| End | Reggie White |
| | Clyde Simmons |
| Tackle | Jerome Brown |
| | Andy Harmon |
| Linebacker | Seth Joyner |
| | William Thomas |
| | Jeremiah Trotter |
| Cornerback | Troy Vincent |
| | Bobby Taylor |
| Safety | Brian Dawkins |
| | Andre Waters |
| Kicker | Roger Ruzek |
| Kick returner | Vai Sikahema |

# When McNabb Touched Down

Philadelphia fans were not thrilled when their team drafted Syracuse quarterback and Chicago native Donovan McNabb in 1999, even though his résumé certainly warranted the selection.

McNabb was a four-year starter at Syracuse and also played on their nationally ranked basketball team. He had been named the Big East Conference's offensive player of the decade and the conference's offensive player of the year an unprecedented three times from 1996 to 1998, as well as the first-team all-conference quarterback in each of his four seasons.

He set Syracuse and Big East career records for touchdown passes (77), total touchdowns (96), passing yards (8,389), total offensive yards (9,950), and total offensive plays (1,403). McNabb also held the school's all-time records for total yards per game (221.1), passing efficiency (155.1), and yards per attempt. He started every game during his career at Syracuse and compiled a 33–12 record.

What else could Philly fans want? Ricky Williams. That's what they wanted, the high-profile Heisman Trophy winner. But since the day McNabb was drafted, fans watched the 6'2", 240-pound quarterback rewrite nearly all the passing records for the franchise. He led them to four straight winning seasons, four NFC East titles, and an NFC championship.

One could make the case that he is the greatest quarterback in Eagles history. But until he has a Super Bowl championship to his credit, that may be a claim open to dispute.

There is no dispute about the numbers, though. McNabb has registered some of the best seasons ever by any Philadelphia passer: 3,233 yards and 25 touchdowns in 2001 and 3,875 yards, 31 touchdowns, and

That Wilma McNabb has become the most familiar sports mom in America because of the Chunky Soup campaign that showed her handing out soup to Donovan and the rest of his teammates? She's even had a Gatorade bucket dumped on her! "People ask for my autograph, but sometimes I tell them I only sign cans of Chunky Soup—because I know that they don't have a Chunky Soup can in their pocket," Wilma said. She and her husband Sam are active in the league in their own way. Wilma, a registered nurse, is vice president of the Professional Football Mothers Association, while Sam, an electrical engineer, is the founder of the NFL Father's Association.

just six interceptions in 2004. In seven seasons, McNabb has thrown for 19,433 yards and 134 touchdowns. Even in 2005, having missed seven games because of a severe abdominal muscle pull, McNabb still threw for 2,507 yards and 16 touchdown passes. And, save for the one year Terrell Owens was on the field and functional, McNabb has worked with a less-than-stellar receiving corps.

Off the field, he has become one of the most popular and recognizable players in the league, and he is one of the athletic leaders in the city of Philadelphia. He has gained national attention with the television ads featuring him and his mother Wilma in the Campbell's Chunky Soup commercials. He has committed himself to a number of charitable ventures, including the Donovan McNabb Foundation, which benefits a number of causes, most prominently the American Diabetes Association, for which McNabb is a national spokesman.

When Eagles coach Andy Reid drafted McNabb, he felt he had the right man not just on the field, but off as well. "I thought he was probably best wired to fit into the city of Philadelphia," Reid said. "There were other quarterbacks who were going to be good quarterbacks—I'm not going to take anything away from them—but his personality would fit best in Philadelphia."

But his star was tarnished by the feud in which he found himself with Owens. As the 2005 season began, the trash-talking receiver, who was battling the organization and refusing to report to camp because he was unhappy with his contract, declared that if the Eagles had a quarterback like Brett Favre, they would be a better team. "A number of commentators will say he's a warrior, he's played with injuries," Owens said,

*Donovan McNabb has been rewriting the passing records for the Philadelphia Eagles since his rookie season in 1999 and has set a number of team records, including most passes completed in a season, with 330 in 2000.*

That Donovan McNabb was so sick in the huddle during Super Bowl XXXIX that he threw up? That unfortunate occurrence put him in an "elite" group of public figures who have lost their lunches at inopportune moments—figures such as former President George Bush, who threw up in the lap of a Japanese government official, and former heavyweight champion Larry Holmes, who lost his lunch in the corner during his title fight against Evander Holyfield.

referring to Favre. "I feel like him being knowledgeable about the quarterback position, I feel like we'd probably be in a better situation."

McNabb shot back that he felt Owens's comments were an insult to him not just as a quarterback, but as a black athlete, and also said he never felt the receiver's apology for the comments he made was sincere.

Owens was suspended and sent home because of his ongoing battle with the team halfway through the 2005 season, but McNabb's reputation was damaged in the process. There was a perception that the team was divided between McNabb and Owens.

But there has been no shortage of teammates who have been willing to testify to McNabb's leadership abilities. "He's always carried himself with class," safety Brian Dawkins said. "I guess it's the best that you could ask a person to handle all the adversity he's had. And then he's definitely a leader when it comes to the team. Guys listen to him. Young guys ask him questions, and he's always there. And he's also a guy who can keep everything loose. He's not timid, and he doesn't tense up. So all those things contribute to him being one of the leaders of this team." Center Hank Fraley has no problems with McNabb leading his team. "I believe Donovan McNabb is one of the best quarterbacks to ever play the game," Fraley said. "He's a great leader. He lets his play do his talking. He'll let people take their own opinion away. He has one focus: to win and be a great teammate."

With Owens gone, McNabb was more determined to get back to the business of winning a Super Bowl. "I play this game to be the best," he said. "And the only sure way I know to be the best is to outwork everybody else. Some people take one step toward their dream, accomplish a little something, and then feel like that's it. Not me. I'm never satisfied."

One of the criticisms of McNabb is that he has failed to win the big game. But he has a long list of games where he took the team on his shoulders and pulled out important victories, including the January 11, 2004, NFC divisional playoff game against Green Bay. In that contest McNabb led the Eagles back after being down 14–0 in the first quarter. With 2:21 remaining, he took over at the Eagles' own 20-yard line and began a dramatic game-tying drive, which included a fourth-and-26 completion to Freddie Mitchell to keep the drive alive. David Akers would later kick a 37-yard field goal to send the game into overtime and then hit a 31-yard kick to win it.

One year earlier, also against Green Bay on *Monday Night Football*, McNabb orchestrated a memorable two-minute drill to defeat the Packers at Lambeau Field. Down 14–10 with 2:43 remaining, he drove the Eagles 65 yards in eight plays, which culminated in a six-yard touchdown pass to Todd Pinkston.

Both of those victories, it should be noted, came against Brett Favre.

# Missing Link Found?

Both Philadelphia Eagles officials and fans felt they needed something or someone to get the team over the hurdle they had bumped up against for three straight years—the NFC title game. Club officials decided the best candidate available was one of the most talented and controversial receivers in the league—Terrell Owens.

There was only one problem—he wasn't available.

Owens *had* been available. He had wanted out of San Francisco, and the 49ers wanted to get rid of him. But Owens believed he was a free agent and therefore had no intention of going along with being traded by the 49ers to the Baltimore Ravens in exchange for a second-round draft choice. Owens didn't want to play in Baltimore. He wanted to play in Philadelphia, with a star quarterback like Donovan McNabb who could get him the ball, and for a team that was on the brink of reaching the Super Bowl, like the Eagles.

The four-time Pro Bowl receiver was supposed to become a free agent on March 3, 2004. But his agent failed to file papers voiding the final years of his contract by a February 21 deadline. The 49ers then traded Owens to the Ravens on March 4—*after* Owens had agreed to a contract with the Eagles that reportedly included a $10-million signing bonus. Owens protested the trade to the Ravens, refused to show up for a physical, and insisted he wanted to play for the Eagles. The union filed a grievance on Owens's behalf, asking that the league declare him a free agent, and the case was set to go before an arbitrator. But before a ruling could be made, a settlement was reached that sent Owens to Philadelphia, where he signed a seven-year deal. The Eagles sent a fifth-round draft pick to Baltimore and defensive end Brandon Whiting to San

Francisco, while the Ravens got back the second-round pick they had traded to the 49ers.

Owens has averaged 93 receptions, 1,316 yards, and 13 touchdowns from 2002 through 2005—one of the biggest impact players a team could have on its offense. In 2003 he caught 80 passes for 1,102 yards and nine touchdowns—his lowest totals since 1999.

But there were questions about whether the rewards were worth the headaches—Owens was also seen as perhaps the most difficult and controversial player in the NFL. Two years previously he had pulled out a pen and signed a ball after scoring a touchdown in Seattle—a serious no-no. He wasn't fined for the move, but he was severely chastised by Commissioner Paul Tagliabue, who said Owens would be disciplined for any such future stunts. Owens also caused a fight once during a game by dancing on the Dallas Cowboys' star at midfield at Texas Stadium after scoring. He constantly bickered with his teammates, once insulting his quarterback, Jeff Garcia. During the 2003 season he threw a sideline tantrum in a game against Cleveland and lost it again the following week against Minnesota, chewing out offensive coordinator Greg Knapp.

Owens was not the only newcomer. The Eagles also signed defensive end Jevon Kearse, who brought a star presence to the defense as well—though his was a more calming presence than Owens's. They needed the addition on that side of the ball, as they had lost their two Pro Bowl cornerbacks, Troy Vincent and Bobby Taylor, to free agency.

Everything looked good for Owens and the Eagles as they opened the 2004 season with a 31–17 win over the New York Giants at Lincoln Financial Field. Owens caught three touchdown passes from McNabb—a

**By the NUMBERS** **.657**—Despite the bitter feelings caused by the Super Bowl loss, one could make the case that there has never been a better coach in the history of the franchise than Andy Reid. Before the start of the 2005 season Reid had the highest winning percentage of any coach in club history, with an overall record of 71–37, a .657 percentage. He also has more playoff wins than any coach in club history. But Greasy Neale had two world championships, while Buck Shaw also had one, and in football, that is how the best are often measured.

20-yarder, a three-yard toss, and a 12-yard pass—while running back Brian Westbrook, now the team's go-to running back with the departure of Duce Staley, rushed for 119 yards, his first career 100-yard rushing game. McNabb completed 26 of 36 passes for 330 yards and four touchdowns.

The success continued, as the Eagles lost only one game—a 27–3 defeat at the hands of the Pittsburgh Steelers—while posting 13 wins. Owens was magnificent, setting a league record with seven straight 100-yard-plus games receiving. Then the hopes and dreams of Eagles fans seemed to come crashing down when Owens broke his right ankle in a 12–7 win over the Dallas Cowboys on December 19 before the home fans. It was a devastating blow with Owens seemingly done for the season. "I was looking forward to the playoffs, really trying to get this team to the Super Bowl," Owens told reporters. "I think without me, still, they will achieve that goal. There's no reason for the city of Philadelphia to get down because I'm not there. Obviously, my presence will be missed, but we have the guys to get it done."

Fortunately for the Eagles, they had already clinched the NFC East and home-field advantage throughout the playoffs, so they coasted in the final two weeks of the regular season, losing 20–7 to the Rams in St. Louis and 38–10 to Cincinnati at home. They would get a first-round bye. Going into the divisional playoff game against the Minnesota Vikings, there was talk that Owens might be able to make it back in time for the Super Bowl—if the team made it that far. Most of the talk was coming from Owens, though, as many observers remained skeptical that he could return in time without risking long-term injury.

Obviously, if the Eagles lost in the NFC playoffs, the question of Owens's return was moot. His teammates played hard, determined to keep the question—and their playoff hopes—alive. They defeated the Vikings 27–14, with McNabb completing 21 of 31 passes for 286 yards and two touchdowns and David Akers hitting two field goals.

There was speculation going into the NFC championship game that the league's newest superstar, Atlanta Falcons quarterback Michael Vick, would be too much for the Eagles defense to handle. But defensive coordinator Jimmy Johnson's unit was all over Vick, holding him to only 103 yards passing, with one interception. Meanwhile the offense, led by Westbrook, Dorsey Levens, and McNabb, controlled the ball with a

When All-Pro receiver Terrell Owens arrived in Philadelphia in 2004 , he paid
immediate dividends, setting a league record with seven straight 100-yard-plus
games receiving.

*Terrell Owens came back from a broken ankle to play in the Super Bowl—a 24–21 loss to the New England Patriots—and criticized his team's play after the game, causing friction between him and quarterback Donovan McNabb.*

rushing game that gained 156 yards on 33 carries, controlling the ball and the game in a 27–10 win—an historic one for coach Andy Reid. The Eagles had finally won the NFC championship and were on their way to the Super Bowl for the first time in 24 years.

Now all the focus was on whether or not Owens would play. Newspaper columnists across the country thought he was foolish to try, and the team was cautious in how they handled the decision. But they left the possibility open right up to game time. When the Eagles offense finally lined up on Sunday, February 6, 2005, at Alltel Stadium against the defending Super Bowl champion New England Patriots, Terrell Owens lined up with them—despite screws and a plate in his right ankle.

Philadelphia blew an early scoring opportunity when they had the ball on the Patriots' 8-yard line in the first quarter. But McNabb was sacked for a 16-yard loss by linebacker Mike Vrabel, and then Rodney Harrison intercepted a McNabb pass at the 3-yard line. The score remained 0–0 going into the second quarter. Philadelphia got on the board first with a nine-play, 80-yard drive that ended with a six-yard pass to tight end L.J. Smith. The Patriots came back to tie the game at 7–7 with a four-yard pass from Tom Brady to David Givens, and the game remained tied going into halftime. In the third quarter, after converting two third-and-long situations, New England scored on a two-yard pass from Brady to Vrabel, who had been inserted as a tight end in the goal-line offense. Philadelphia answered right back with McNabb leading a 10-play, 74-yard drive, tying the game again at 14–14 with a 10-yard scoring pass to Westbrook.

With the score tied going into the fourth quarter, the game became a 15-minute contest. The Patriots were up to it; the Eagles were not. New England scored 10 points in five minutes on a two-yard run by Corey Dillon and a 22-yard field goal by Adam Vinatieri. With five minutes and 40 seconds left, the Eagles got the football on their own 21-yard line, and McNabb led a 13-play, 79-yard drive that concluded with a 30-yard touchdown pass to wide receiver Greg Lewis, cutting the Patriots' lead to 24–21 with 1:48 left in the game. New England's Christian Fauria recovered an onside kick attempt by Philadelphia, but the Eagles defense forced a punt. Dexter Reid downed Josh Miller's 32-yard punt at the

That part of Donovan McNabb's preparation during the off-season includes vision training? To help his eyes process information at a faster rate, McNabb dons a pair of "strobe specs" or "Star Trek glasses" (as McNabb calls them) and goes through simulated football situations such as finding receivers or picking up oncoming blitzers. "The good quarterbacks are probably like fighter pilots," said Coach Andy Reid. "You always heard Ted Williams talk about this with his hitting. The fighter pilots have that extra sense of feeling about what's going on around them and then they can react calmly in stressful times."

Eagles' 4-yard line with 46 seconds left, and Harrison intercepted a McNabb pass three plays later to clinch the title.

But it wasn't as simple as that. Reid received heavy criticism for his poor clock management in the final five minutes of the game, and then there was the controversy swirling around McNabb, who froze in the huddle in the final minutes and, according to several teammates, got sick on the field, perhaps from a hit he took earlier in the game, or perhaps because of exhaustion. He finished the game, completing 30 of 51 passes for 357 yards and three touchdowns, with three interceptions. For his part, Owens was magnificent, catching nine passes for 122 yards.

There was a hint of bitterness in Owens's words in the locker room after the loss. "We were too sloppy to win," he said. "It was great to get back, but we made too many mistakes. We could have won, and that hurts."

McNabb had an MVP season, completing 300 of 469 passes for 3,875 yards and 31 touchdowns with only eight interceptions; he finished second to Marshall Faulk in the Associated Press MVP Voting. There were countless other honors—he was named NFL Player of the Year by CBS Radio, was a three-time NFC Player of the Month, and was voted offensive MVP by his teammates.

But none of it was good enough for Owens, who caught 77 passes for 1,200 yards and 14 touchdowns. That hint of bitterness after the Super Bowl would emerge as an enormous problem that would engulf the entire franchise in the coming year.

# As the World Turns

The Philadelphia Eagles finished with a 6–10 record in 2005, and were shut out of the playoffs for the first time since 1999. It was perhaps one of the most embarrassing seasons in the history of the franchise, even though there were Philadelphia teams that had finished with far worse records over the years. But off-the-field controversies turned the season into something like a soap opera, with who else but Terrell Owens at the center of it all.

It didn't start out that way. Philadelphia won four of its first six games, with several inspiring victories, including a dramatic come-from-behind win at Kansas City in which the Eagles, down 27–6 in the first half, came back to win 37–31. It appeared that the Eagles were worthy defenders of their NFC championship.

But it was all an illusion. The Eagles went on to lose eight of their final 10 games. A number of key players were hurt and missed large chunks of playing time, including Donovan McNabb (with a sports hernia), Brian Westbrook (with a foot injury), Hank Fraley (with a torn rotator cuff), Todd Pinkston (with an Achilles tendon injury), Lito Sheppard (with an ankle injury), and Tra Thomas (with a back injury). But physical injuries weren't really the cause of the Eagles' pitiful 2005 season. A bigger problem was the stress caused by the battle that All-Pro wide receiver Owens engaged in with the club and with his quarterback. All anyone will remember about the 2005 Eagles will be the turmoil caused by Owens and the price the franchise wound up paying for taking on such a talented—but troubled—player in their quest to win a Super Bowl championship.

It began when Owens took a verbal swipe at McNabb's performance in the Super Bowl. McNabb responded harshly and the two feuded, not

*Running back Brian Westbrook, an unknown out of nearby Villanova University, has been a double threat, rushing for 2,235 yards and gaining 1,737 yards receiving since his 2002 rookie season.*

speaking to each other throughout the summer. Owen also demanded that his seven-year, $48.97-million contract, signed in March 2004, be renegotiated—a conflict that turned into the biggest soap opera in the NFL and made nightly news in Philadelphia.

First Owens refused to come to training camp. Then, when he finally did arrive, he refused to speak to McNabb, who tried to stay above the fray, but couldn't help but be dragged down into it. Said McNabb:

> I choose to be amused because I have a job to do. I won't let one person or one thing take me away from one of my goals, and my goal is obviously to win the Super Bowl. In order for me to do that, I have to make sure I'm clicking on all cylinders, I'm focused on the task at hand, and making sure I'm getting all 11 guys in the right positions. I can't focus on what people are saying on the outside or take time out of a series or take time out of a practice to dwell on what's been negative in the past couple of days.

Although McNabb struggled to keep a positive attitude, the conflict would last far longer than a couple of days. The Eagles sent Owens home from camp after a few days for his conduct, and when he returned, the team could not escape the turmoil.

Owens raised the tension to a new level when he criticized the organization for not honoring him after he caught his 100th career touchdown pass. Then he commented that if the Eagles had Brett Favre, they would be undefeated. Now the team was engulfed in the chaos of T.O., and a half-hearted apology did little to appease the team, which decided to suspend him.

His second apology—issued a few days later from his home in Moorestown, New Jersey, with an army of media on hand and his controversial agent, Drew Rosenhaus, at his side—wasn't much better. Begging for his reinstatement, Owens claimed, "This is very painful for me, to be in this position. I know in my heart I can help this team win a Super Bowl, not only being a dominant player but being a team player. The mentality that I have, my greatest strength, can also be my greatest weakness. I'm a fighter. I've always been and I'll always be. I fight for what I think is right. In doing so, I alienated a lot of my fans and my teammates."

The Best Ever

These are the best to ever play for the Philadelphia Eagles from 1933 to 2005, with a championship victory serving as the deciding factor in close decisions.

| Position | Name |
|---|---|
| Coach | Greasy Neale |
| *Offense* | |
| Wide receiver | Pete Pihos |
| | Harold Carmichael |
| Tight end | Pete Retzlaff |
| Tackle | Jerry Sisemore |
| | Stan Walters |
| Guard | Bucko Kilroy |
| | Woody Peoples |
| Center | Guy Morriss |
| Running back | Wilbert Montgomery |
| | Steve Van Buren |
| Quarterback | Norm Van Brocklin |
| *Defense* | |
| End | Reggie White |
| | Clyde Simmons |
| Tackle | Jerome Brown |
| | Charlie Johnson |
| Linebacker | Chuck Bednarik |
| | Bill Bergey |
| | Seth Joyner |
| Cornerback | Eric Allen |
| | Herman Edwards |
| Safety | Bill Bradley |
| | Andre Waters |
| Kicker | David Akers |
| Kick returner | Brian Westbrook |

"He [Owens] needs to be playing," said Rosenhaus. "We hope he plays again for the Philadelphia Eagles. We hope he plays right away." But those pleas fell on deaf ears. The suspension issued by the Eagles was upheld by an arbitrator, and the team punished the receiver further by telling him to stay home for the rest of the season after his four-game suspension was over. "He was told not to return because of a large number of situations that accumulated over a long period of time," Coach Andy Reid said.

Looking back on the season, the player the Eagles seemed to miss most was not Owens, but Westbrook, as the offense had virtually no running game. Their passing offense ranked eighth in the league, while their rushing offense finished 28th, averaging only 89.5 yards per game.

Against this ugly backdrop, one moment of honor did take place. Reggie White's No. 92 was officially retired after White unexpectedly died of a heart attack at the age of 43. The emotional halftime ceremony, which took place during a *Monday Night Football* contest versus Seattle on December 5, included White's wife, Sara, and their two children, as well as more than 20 of his former teammates and coaches. It was the perfect time to remember a player who brought pride and glory to the city and its fans, in the middle of a year in which everyone was consumed by another player who brought Philadelphia embarrassment and shame.

The Eagles concluded their 2005 season with a 31–20 loss to Washington that was a mirror image of the year's campaign. There were some good plays, but the Eagles committed six turnovers—just too many mistakes to overcome. Reid stood before reporters and took responsibility for the collapse, but he refused to second guess any of the team's decisions about Owens:

> I made the decision and went with it—to bring him here and then to sit him down. That is what I did and I am not going to look back on it and say I wish I would have done either ors. I don't do that.
>
> We didn't play well enough. With our record, I don't think I did very well. I have to do a better job—it starts with me.

**GOLD STANDARD**

## The Cadillac of Receivers

Terrell Owens's stay with the Philadelphia Eagles was brief and tumultuous, but he nevertheless left his mark on the franchise record books. In 2004 he set team records for single-season touchdown catches, with 14; for single-season 100-yard receiving games, with seven; and consecutive 100-yard games, with five. He is also the only player in the history of the franchise with the middle name of Eldorado.

You have to dig in and go. You have to take care of business, everybody has to work a little harder, and good things will happen. This can all be switched around and made into excuses and it should not be. I don't want it to be that way, but we have not had quite this many guys banged up.

Hopefully, those guys will come back and contribute like they did before they were hurt. We didn't have that that first year. That was not the situation. You get out there and you have to evaluate why things are not working.

On March 14, 2006, the Eagles took care of one thing that wasn't working, finally releasing Owens. Wherever the team might now be headed, they would at least not be hampered by the histrionics of a player who never quite delivered on his potential.

# Not Even Santa Is Safe

There are some football fans out there with reputations that strike fear into the hearts of opposing fans and players alike: the Oakland Raiders faithful, the Cleveland Browns diehards, and, of course, Philadelphia Eagles fans.

Eagles fans are considered among the most passionate and notorious in professional football, as well as having a claim to fame that no other fan base can call its own: they once booed Santa Claus. That December day in 1968 at Franklin Field forever defined the identity of Eagles fans.

The Philly faithful were suffering from years of losing and the frustration that comes with it. They had targeted head coach Joe Kuharich as the cause of their misery, raining boos down on him at home games along with chants of "Joe Must Go." By the time the 2–11 Eagles played their final game of the 1968 season against the Minnesota Vikings at home on December 15, the fans had had their fill and were looking for someone to take it out on.

Along came Santa Claus, in the form of a 20-year-old kid named Frank Olivo. He had been wearing a Santa suit and a fake white beard to the last Eagles home game of the season for several years. As halftime approached, the Eagles' entertainment director asked Olivo to replace a hired Santa stranded by the snowstorm. As instructed, Olivo ran downfield past a row of elf-costumed "Eaglettes" and the team's 50-musician brass band playing "Here Comes Santa Claus." The crowd roared with boos, followed by snowballs. "When I hit the end zone, and the snowballs started, I was waving my finger at the crowd, saying 'You're not getting anything for Christmas,'" Olivo recalled.

*Eagles fans are among the most passionate in professional football. Their reputation has made them feared among visiting players and fans alike.*
Photo courtesy of AP/Wide World Photos.

That Eagles fans aren't the only ones with a reputation for toughness in Philadelphia? Basketball fans booed hometown star Kobe Bryant when he came to town for the 2002 NBA All-Star Game. And Phillies fans threw D-cell batteries at St. Louis Cardinals outfielder J.D. Drew, who held out for a year after the Phillies drafted him and eventually signed with the Cardinals instead.

After Howard Cosell repeated the story on his national radio show, it became part of the mystique of Eagles fans. "It became a thing that Philadelphia sports fans became famous for doing," Olivo said. That game turned out to be Kuharich's swan song, as he was fired at the end of the season. He, too, had been pelted with snowballs that day as his team came off the field at halftime in a 24–17 loss to Minnesota.

The team moved to Veterans Stadium in 1971, and the reputation of Eagles fans only grew with more tales of outrageous behavior. They even adopted their own section in the stadium—the 700 section—which came to be known as "the Nest of Death."

"We like to put the fear of God in most teams and the fans that come into the stadium," said Bill Deery, a season-ticket holder who sat in the 700 section. "One time during a Redskins game, there was some guy wearing a Riggins [John Riggins, Redskins running back] jersey and a pigskin mask. The Redskins were beating the Eagles bad, and this guy would just not sit down and shut up. The next thing you knew, four Eagles fans were giving the guy an early exit."

Eagles fans were so tough and out of control sometimes that the city actually opened up a jail—complete with a court and a judge—inside Veterans Stadium after a particularly nasty bout of drunkenness and fighting at a *Monday Night Football* game between the Eagles and the 49ers in 1997. Former Redskins kicker Mark Moseley, who had the first kickoff ever at the new stadium when he was still playing for the Eagles, didn't look forward to playing there. "It was always a tough place to play," he said. "The crowd was always rowdy and nasty—some very rough people. One time I got hit in the head with a bottle. It was a good thing I had my helmet on."

This wasn't a reputation that Eagles management was particularly proud of, and in the final days of the Vet, when there was much attention

DID YOU KNOW . . . That the infamous reputation of Philadelphia sports fans has gone beyond the playing field and now inspires the theater as well? Tom McCarthy, a lifelong Philadelphia sports fan, wrote, acted, and produced a one-man show called "Philly Fan," a play that depicts the long history of disappointment, frustration, and anguish that comes with being a fan of professional sports in Philadelphia. "It's not a real stretch. ... I've had my heart broken many times," said McCarthy.

focused on the Nest of Death, officials did all they could to stop the media from covering the story. During one *Monday Night Football* game, reporters from *The Press of Atlantic City* and KYW radio in Philadelphia were removed from the section, where they were interviewing fans. Their tape recorders were confiscated. The *Press* reporter was held in the stadium's police station while the KYW reporter was escorted from the premises. Eagles management felt the need for this strict control because a tabloid television crew had secretly followed Veterans Stadium security guards trying to keep order in the 700 section during the previous week.

Contrary to what some might expect, this rowdy group wasn't always made up of society's bottom-feeders. The sometimes out-of-control passion of Eagles fans crosses all sorts of class lines. In 1989 a huge ice and snowstorm hit Philadelphia on December 8. There was still a lot of snow in the stands by the time of the December 10 game against Dallas at the Vet—snow that would only serve as ammunition for Eagles fans. Philadelphia was winning 20–10 in the fourth quarter when a lawyer sitting up in the 700 section began taking bets that nobody could hit the Cowboys bench with a snowball from that distance. Soon the police were involved, and after the game Jimmy Johnson needed an escort through all the snowballs being thrown. The incident drew national attention, particularly when it was revealed in *The Philadelphia Inquirer* that the instigator was an attorney by the name of Edward G. Rendell—the city's district attorney. Two years later Rendell was elected mayor of Philadelphia, and he is now governor of Pennsylvania.

Rendell paid off on a $20 bet he made with his cohorts and later apologized when the story hit the papers. "I assume they used my $20 to buy beer," he said. Rendell has also said that he was in the stands for the Santa Claus game, and he explains the booing like this: "Most of the time, they're [Eagles fans] not really as tough as they seem. They boo players who don't make an effort."

Apparently that includes players who can't even move as well. In 1999 fans jeered Cowboys receiver Michael Irvin as he lay on the field for 20 minutes, suffering from a neck injury that ended his career.

Whatever criticisms Eagles fans may face from the rest of the civilized world, there is no disputing their loyalty to their team. The franchise has drawn between 500,000 and 700,000 fans every year for the last 25 seasons. It remains to be seen if this passion will sustain itself in the team's new home, Lincoln Financial Field. Perhaps the team's recent winning ways—even with the frustration of failing to win a Super Bowl— have softened Eagles fans enough that Santa Claus might once again be safe.

# ANSWERS TO
# TRIVIA QUESTIONS

**Page 5:** The Yellow Jackets got into a battle with the Pottsville Maroons, who had scheduled a game against the Notre Dame All-Stars (featuring the famous Four Horsemen)—a game that would be played in the Yellow Jackets' territory. Frankford officials filed a protest with the league, arguing they had a game scheduled against Notre Dame the same day at Frankford Stadium. League President Joe Carr supported Frankford's protest and ordered Pottsville to cancel the Notre Dame game. But the Maroons played the game anyway, and Carr suspended the franchise.

**Page 11:** By 1934 only one small-town team remained in the NFL. Frankford's move from the outskirts of the city into Philadelphia in 1933 represented a league trend at the time, as the game sought to change from a small-town attraction to become a big-city sporting event. In 1925 the league had teams in places like Rock Island, Illinois; Providence, Rhode Island; Hammond, Indiana; Duluth, Minnesota; and Rochester, New York. By 1933 none of those teams were still in the league; the sport's fan base had become more urban, leaving only Green Bay, Wisconsin, and Portsmouth, Ohio, with small-town teams. The Portsmouth team abandoned that location at the end of the 1933 season.

**Page 15:** Paul Crewe is the name of the fictional character who led a prison football team in Robert Altman's film *The Longest Yard*. Alabama Pitts was his day's version of Crewe. Organized sports teams were far more prevalent in prisons in the 1930s than they are now. Most prison football programs play only flag football, although Angola State Prison in Louisiana still has the full-contact version.

**Page 21:** Philadelphia receiver Joe Carter led the NFL in pass receptions in 1934, catching 16 for 238 yards and four touchdowns, even though the team finished with a 4–7 record.

**Page 25:** The Eagles' record in their first decade was 18-55-3. Though they were founded in the 1930s, fans had to be glad to see the decade end and 1940 arrive—the franchise had been the worst in the league since it began play in 1933.

**Page 32:** Eagles receiver Don Looney's son is running back Joe Don Looney. Don Looney played for the Eagles for just one season, in 1940, but he made an impact, catching 58 passes for 707 yards, an NFL record at the time. His son followed in his footsteps to the NFL, but eccentric running back Joe Don Looney, considered one of the most talented but troubled players the league has ever seen, marched to the beat of a different drummer once he got there.

**Page 43:** Allie Sherman played five seasons at quarterback for the Eagles before becoming a very successful NFL head coach. One of the smallest players ever to play quarterback for the Eagles, Sherman joined the team in 1943. At only 5'11" and 160 pounds, Sherman somehow managed to survive for five seasons in the league, although he never distinguished himself at quarterback. Instead he would leave his mark as a successful coach for the New York Giants, winning three NFC East titles from 1961 to 1963 and compiling a record of 57–51–4 over eight seasons.

**Page 48:** Steven Van Buren had eight consecutive 100-yard games in 1947, which is still a franchise record.

**Page 53:** Opposing teams scored 17 first-quarter points against the Eagles in 1948. The championship squad had an outstanding defense, allowing only 156 points over 12 games. They clamped down especially hard during first quarters.

**Page 61:** When asked about the legendary hit he put on New York Giants superstar (and later *Monday Night Football* fixture) Frank Gifford, Chuck Bednarik joked with the reporter that, "I wish it was Kathie Lee on that shot instead of Frank."

**Page 66:** Eagles quarterback Adrian Burk shares the NFL record for the most touchdown passes thrown in a single game. Burk won his share of the record (which still stands today) on October 17, 1954, when he threw seven touchdown passes in a 49–21 win over the Redskins at Griffith Stadium in Washington, D.C., tying the mark set by Sid Luckman in 1943.

**Page 71:** Eight players on the 1960 Eagles championship team were named to the Pro Bowl: linebackers Chuck Bednarik and Maxie Baughan; cornerback Tom Brookshier; tackle (and future head coach) Marion Campbell; wide receiver Tommy McDonald; tight end Pete Retzlaff; quarterback Norm Van Brocklin; and kicker Bobby Walston.

**Page 88:** The Eagles had no Pro Bowl representative in 1970. The 3–10–1 squad was so bad that they were shut out of the Pro Bowl—the only time in the history of the game that the franchise did not have a representative in the NFL's All-Star Game.

**Page 95:** Wilbert Montgomery, who was drafted in 1976 out of Abilene Christian, is the franchise leader in 100-yard rushing games, having run for 100 yards 26 times in his career. Steve Van Buren is next with 19, followed by Duce Staley with 13, and Ricky Watters with 12.

**Page 103:** The franchise record for attendance in a single season is 557,325 fans. The 1980 NFC champion Eagles drew that many faithful to the Vet over eight regular-season home games. That squad was one of the all-time most popular among Eagles fans, and it showed at the turnstiles.

**Page 117:** Quarterback Scott Tinsley threw for 338 yards in a 41–22 loss to the Cowboys in 1987. The Eagles didn't field a very good replacement team for the three games in which NFL players were on strike after week two of the 1987 season, losing all three games. But the star of Philadelphia's strike team had to be Tinsley, who completed 24 of 34 passes for three touchdowns in a loss in which a number of NFL players crossed the picket line.

**Page 126:** The Detmer brothers both played quarterback and were on the Eagles' roster at the same time. The Eagles love the Detmer family, so much so that they are the only franchise in NFL history to have quarterback brothers on the roster at the same time. Ty Detmer was the Eagles' starting quarterback in 1996, passing for 2,911 yards and 15 touchdowns. The franchise drafted Ty's brother Koy in 1997—the last year Ty was with the Eagles. Koy has remained a backup on the team for the past nine seasons.

**Page 129:** Before purchasing the Eagles from Norman Braman in 1994, Jeff Lurie was involved in the high-profile business of movie making. Much was made, at the time, of Lurie's background as a film producer but he proved to be a better football executive than a Hollywood mogul. His production company, Chestnut Hill Productions, was not exactly the second coming of MGM Studios. They only produced two films of note—*Sweet Hearts Dance* with Don Johnson and *I Love You to Death* with Kevin Kline—neither of which was a box office hit.

# Philadephia Eagles All-Time Roster (through 2005 season)

The following players have been on the Eagles active roster for at least one regular or postseason game during the years indicated. In addition, players who spent the entire year on the injured reserve list since 1993 and thus have accrued an NFL season are also listed.

† Denotes replacement players during the 1987 strike

**A**

| | |
|---|---|
| Abercrombie, Walter (RB), Baylor | 1988 |
| Absher, Dick (LB), Maryland | 1972 |
| Adams, Gary (DB), Arkansas | 1969 |
| Adams, Keith (LB), Clemson | 2002 |
| Adams, Theo (G), Hawaii | 1995 |
| Agajanian, Ben (G), New Mexico | 1945 |
| Akers, David (K), Louisville | 1999 |
| Alexander, David (C), Tulsa | 1987–94 |
| Alexander, Kermit (DB), UCLA | 1972–73 |
| Allen, Chuck (LB), Washington | 1972 |
| Allen, Eric (CB), Arizona State | 1988–94 |
| Allen, Ian (T), Purdue | 2004 |
| Allen, Jackie (DB), Baylor | 1972 |
| Allen, Kevin (T), Indiana | 1985 |
| Allert, Ty (LB), Texas | 1987–89 |
| Allison, Henry (G), San Diego State | 1971–72 |
| Amerson, Glen (B), Texas Tech | 1961 |
| Amundson, George (RB), Iowa State | 1975 |
| Anderson, Gary (K), Syracuse | 1995–96 |
| Andrews, Leroy (B), Kansas State Teachers College of Pittsburgh | 1934 |
| Andrews, Shawn (T/G), Arkansas | 2004 |

| | |
|---|---|
| Angelo, Jim (G), Indiana (Pennsylvania) † | 1987 |
| Antwine, Houston (DT), Southern Illinois | 1972 |
| Archer, Dave (QB), Iowa State | 1991–92 |
| Armour, Justin (WR), Stanford | 1997 |
| Armstrong, Harvey (DT), Southern Methodist University | 1982–84 |
| Armstrong, Neill (E), Oklahoma A&M | 1947–51 |
| Arnold, Jay (B), Texas | 1937–40 |
| Arrington, Rick (QB), Tulsa | 1970–73 |
| Aschbacher, Darrel (G), Oregon | 1959 |
| Asher, Jamie (TE), Louisville | 1999 |
| Atkins, Steve (FB), Maryland | 1981 |
| Auer, Howard (T), Michigan | 1933 |
| Auer, Jim (DE), Georgia† | 1987 |
| Autry, Darnell (RB), Northwestern | 1998, 2000 |
| Ayers, Marvin (DE), Grambling† | 1987 |

**B**

| | |
|---|---|
| Bahr, Matt (K), Penn State | 1993 |
| Bailey, David (DE), Oklahoma State | 1990 |
| Bailey, Eric (TE), Kansas State† | 1987 |
| Bailey, Howard (T), Tennessee | 1935 |
| Bailey, Tom (B), Florida State | 1971–74 |
| Bailey, Victor (WR), Missouri | 1993–94 |
| Baisi, Albert (G), West Virginia | 1947 |
| Baker, Jason (P), Iowa | 2002 |
| Baker, John (E), North Carolina College | 1962 |
| Baker, Keith (WR), Texas Southern | 1985 |
| Baker, Ron (G), Oklahoma State | 1980–88 |
| Baker, Sam (K), Oregon State | 1964–69 |
| Baker, Tony (B), Iowa State | 1971–72 |

| | |
|---|---|
| Baldinger, Brian (G), Duke | 1992–93 |
| Ballman, Gary (E), Michigan State | 1967–72 |
| Banas, Stephen (B), Notre Dame | 1935 |
| Banducci, Bruno (G), Stanford | 1944–45 |
| Banta, Jack (B), Southern California | 1941, 1944–45 |
| Barber, Shawn (LB), Richmond | 2002 |
| Barker, Bryan (P), Santa Clara | 1994 |
| Barlow, Corey (CB), Auburn | 1992–94 |
| Barnes, Bill (B), Wake Forest | 1957–61 |
| Barnes, Larry (FB), Tennessee State | 1978–79 |
| Barnes, Walter (G), Louisiana State University | 1948–51 |
| Barnett, Fred (WR), Arkansas State | 1990–95 |
| Barnhardt, Dan (B), Centenary | 1934 |
| Barni, Roy (B), University of San Francisco | 1954–55 |
| Barnum, Leonard (B), West Virginia Wesleyan | 1940–42 |
| Barr, Stephen (WR), Pennsylvania | 1965 |
| Bartholomew, Sam (B), Tennessee | 1941 |
| Bartlett, Doug (DT), Northern Illinois | 1988 |
| Bartley, Ephesians (LB), Florida | 1992 |
| Bartrum, Mike (TE/LS), Marshall | 2000 |
| Basca, Nick (B), Villanova | 1941 |
| Bassi, Dick (G), Santa Clara | 1940 |
| Bassman, Herman (B), Ursinus | 1936 |
| Battaglia, Matt (LB), Louisville† | 1987 |
| Baughan, Maxie (LB), Georgia Tech | 1960–65 |
| Bauman, Alfred (T), Northwestern | 1947 |
| Bausch, Frank (C), Kansas | 1940–41 |
| Bavaro, Mark (TE), Notre Dame | 1993–94 |
| Bawel, Bibbles (B), Evansville | 1952, 1955–56 |
| Baze, Winford (B), Texas Tech | 1937 |
| Beach, Pat (TE), Washington State | 1992 |
| Beals, Shawn (WR/KR), Idaho State | 1988 |
| Beaver, Jim (G), Florida | 1962 |
| Beckles, Ian (G), Indiana | 1997–98 |
| Bednarik, Chuck (C/LB), Pennsylvania | 1949–62 |
| Beisler, Randy (DE), Indiana | 1966–68 |
| Bell, Eddie (B), Pennsylvania | 1955–58 |
| Bell, Todd (LB), Ohio State | 1988–89 |
| Bellamy, Mike (WR), Illinois | 1990 |
| Bellamy, Victor (CB), Syracuse† | 1987 |
| Bendross, Jesse (WR), Alabama† | 1987 |
| Benson, Henry (G), West Maryland | 1935 |
| Berger, Mitch (P), Colorado | 1994 |
| Bergey, Bill (LB), Arkansas State | 1974–80 |
| Berry, Dan (B), California | 1967 |
| Berzinski, Willie (B), University of Wisconsin–LaCrosse | 1956 |
| Betterson, James (RB), North Carolina | 1977–78 |
| Bielski, Dick (B), Maryland | 1955–59 |
| Bieniemy, Eric (RB), Colorado | 1999 |
| Binotto, John (B), Duquesne | 1942 |
| Bishop, Blaine (SS), Ball State | 2002 |
| Bjorklund, Robert (C), Minnesota | 1941 |
| Black, Michael (T/G), Sacramento State | 1986 |
| Blackmore, Richard (CB), Mississippi State | 1979–82 |
| Blaine, Ed (G), Missouri | 1963–66 |
| Blake, Jeff (QB), East Carolina | 2004 |
| Bleamer, Jeff (T), Penn State | 1975–76 |
| Bleeker, Mel (B), Southern California | 1944–46 |
| Blue, Luther (WR), Iowa State | 1980 |
| Blye, Ron (RB), Notre Dame | 1969 |
| Boatswain, Harry (G/T), New Haven | 1995, 1997 |
| Boedeker, William (B), DePaul | 1950 |
| Bogren, Vince (E), New Mexico | 1944 |
| Bolden, Gary (DT), Southwest Oklahoma State† | 1987 |
| Boniol, Chris (K), Louisiana Tech | 1997–98 |
| Booty, John (DB), Texas Christian | 1991–92 |
| Boryla, Mike (QB), Stanford | 1974–76 |
| Bostic, James (RB), Auburn | 1998–99 |
| Bostic, Jason (CB), Georgia Tech | 1999–2000 |
| Bouggess, Lee (B), Louisville | 1970–73 |
| Bouie, Kevin (RB), Mississippi State | 1995–96 |
| Bova, Tony (E), St. Francis | 1943 |
| Bowman, Kevin (WR), San Jose State† | 1987 |
| Boykin, Deral (S), Louisville | 1996 |
| Bradley, Bill (FS), Texas | 1969–76 |
| Bradley, Carlos (LB), Wake Forest† | 1987 |
| Bradley, Harold (G), Iowa | 1958 |
| Brady, Rickey (TE), Oklahoma | 1995 |
| Bredice, John (E), Boston University | 1956 |
| Brennan, Leo (T), Holy Cross | 1942 |

| | | | |
|---|---|---|---|
| Brewer, Jack (DB), Minnesota | 2005 | Burks, Dialleo (WR), Eastern Kentucky | 1996 |
| Brewer, John (B), Louisville | 1952–53 | Burnette, Tom (B), North Carolina | 1938 |
| Brian, William (T), Gonzaga | 1935–36 | Burnham, Lem (DE), U.S. International | 1977–80 |
| Bridges, Jeremy (T/G), Southern Mississippi | 2003 | Burnine, Hank (E), Missouri | 1956–57 |
| Brister, Bubby (QB), Northeast Louisiana | 1993–94 | Burroughs, Don (B), Colorado State | 1960–64 |
| Britt, Rankin (E), Texas A&M | 1939 | Bushby, Thomas (B), Kansas State | 1935 |
| Brodnicki, Chuck (T), Temple | 1934 | Buss, Art (T), Michigan State | 1936–37 |
| Brooks, Barrett (T), Kansas State | 1995–98 | Butler, Bob (G), Kentucky | 1962 |
| Brooks, Clifford (DB), Tennessee State | 1975–76 | Butler, John (B), Tennessee | 1943, 1945 |
| Brooks, Tony (RB), Notre Dame | 1992–93 | Byars, Keith (RB), Ohio State | 1986–92 |
| Brookshier, Tom (B), Colorado | 1953, 1956–61 | Byrne, Bill (G), Boston College | 1963 |
| Broughton, Luther (TE), Furman | 1997, 1999–2000 | | |
| Brown, Aaron (LB), Ohio State | 1985 | **C** | |
| Brown, Bob (T), Nebraska | 1964–68 | | |
| Brown, Cedrick (CB), Washington | 1987 | Cabrelli, Larry (E), Colgate | 1941–47 |
| Brown, David (LB), Miami (Ohio) † | 1987 | Caesar, Ivan (LB), Boston College | 1993 |
| Brown, Deauntae (CB), Central State (Ohio) | 1997 | Caffey, Lee Roy (LB), Texas A&M | 1963 |
| Brown, Fred (LB), Miami (Florida) | 1967–69 | Cagle, Jim (DT), Georgia | 1974 |
| Brown, Greg (DE), Kansas State | 1981–86 | Cahill, Dave (DT), Arizona State–Flagstaff | 1966 |
| Brown, Jerome (DT), Miami (Florida) | 1987–91 | Caldwell, Mike (LB), Middle Tennessee | |
| Brown, Na (WR), North Carolina | 1999–2001 | State | 1998–2001 |
| Brown, Reggie (RB), Oregon† | 1987 | Calhoun, Don (RB), Kansas State | 1982 |
| Brown, Reggie (WR), Georgia | 2005 | Calicchio, Lonny (K), Mississippi | 1997 |
| Brown, Sheldon (CB), South Carolina | 2002 | Calloway, Ernie (DT), Texas South | 1969–72 |
| Brown, Thomas (DE), Baylor | 1980 | Campbell, Glenn (E), Emporia Teachers | 1935 |
| Brown, Tim (B), Ball State | 1960–67 | Campbell, Marion (T), Georgia | 1956–61 |
| Brown, Willie (FL), Southern California | 1966 | Campbell, Stan (G), Iowa State | 1959–61 |
| Brumm, Don (DE), Purdue | 1970–71 | Campbell, Tommy (DB), Iowa State | 1976 |
| Brunski, Andrew (C), Temple | 1943 | Campfield, Billy (RB), Kansas | 1978–82 |
| Brutley, Daryon (CB), Northern Iowa | 2003 | Campion, Thomas (T), Southeast Louisiana | 1947 |
| Bryant, Bill (CB), Grambling | 1978 | Canale, Rocco (G), Boston College | 1943–45 |
| Brzezinski, Doug (G), Boston College | 1999–2002 | Carmichael, Harold (WR), Southern | 1971–83 |
| Buckhalter, Correll (RB), Nebraska | 2001 | Carollo, Joe (T), Notre Dame | 1969–70 |
| Budd, Frank (E), Villanova | 1962 | Carpe, Joe (T), Millikin | 1933 |
| Bukant, Joe (B), Washington University | | Carpenter, Rob (WR), Syracuse | 1995 |
| (St. Louis) | 1938–40 | Carr, Earl (RB), Florida | 1979 |
| Bulaich, Norm (RB), Texas Christian | 1973–74 | Carr, Jim (B), Morris Harvey | 1959–63 |
| Bull, Ron (B), Baylor | 1971 | Carrioccio, Russ (G), Virginia | 1955 |
| Bunting, John (LB), North Carolina | 1972–82 | Carroll, Terrence (S), Oregon State | 2001 |
| Burgess, Derrick (LB/DE), Mississippi | 2001–04 | Carson, Carlos (WR), Louisiana State | |
| Burk, Adrian (B), Baylor | 1951–56 | University | 1989 |
| Burke, Mark (DB), West Virginia | 1976 | Carter, Cris (WR), Ohio State | 1987–89 |
| | | Carter, Joe (E), Austin | 1933–40 |

| | | | |
|---|---|---|---|
| Case, Pete (G), Georgia | 1962–64 | Considine, Sean (S), Iowa | 2005 |
| Cassady, Howard (B), Ohio State | 1962 | Conti, Enio (G), Bucknell | 1941–45 |
| Castiglia, Jim (B), Georgetown | 1941, 1945–46 | Conwell, Joe (T), North Carolina | 1986–87 |
| Caterbone, Thomas (CB), Franklin & | | Cook, Leon (T), Northwestern | 1942 |
|    Marsh College† | 1987 | Cook, Rashard (S), Southern California | 1999–2002 |
| Catlin, Tom (LB), Oklahoma | 1959 | Cooke, Ed (E), Maryland | 1958 |
| Cavanaugh, Matt (QB), Pittsburgh | 1986–89 | Cooper, Evan (DB/KR), Michigan | 1984–87 |
| Caver, Quinton (LB), Arkansas | 2001–02 | Cooper, Louis (LB), Western Carolina | 1993 |
| Cemore, Tom (G), Creighton | 1941 | Cooper, Richard (T), Tennessee | 1996–98 |
| Ceppetelli, Gene (C), Villanova | 1968–69 | Copeland, Russell (WR), Memphis State | 1997–98 |
| Chalenski, Mike (DL), UCLA | 1993–95 | Cornish, Frank (C), UCLA | 1995 |
| Chapura, Dick (DT), Missouri | 1990 | Cortez, José (K), Oregon State | 2005 |
| Cheek, Louis (T), Texas A&M | 1990 | Coston, Zed (C), Texas A&M | 1939 |
| Cherry, Je'Rod (S), California | 2000 | Cothren, Paige (B), Mississippi | 1959 |
| Cherundolo, Chuck (C), Penn State | 1940 | Cowher, Bill (LB), North Carolina State | 1983–84 |
| Chesley, Al (LB), Pittsburgh | 1979–82 | Cowhig, Jerry (B), Notre Dame | 1951 |
| Chesson, Wes (WR), Duke | 1973–74 | Crabb, Claude (B), Colorado | 1964–65 |
| Christensen, Jeff (QB), Eastern Illinois | 1984–85 | Craft, Russ (B), Alabama | 1946–53 |
| Chuy, Don (G), Clemson | 1969 | Crafts, Jerry (T/G), Louisville | 1997–98 |
| Cifelli, Gus (T), Notre Dame | 1954 | Crawford, Charles (RB), Oklahoma State | 1986–87 |
| Clark, Al (CB), Eastern Michigan | 1976 | Creech, Bob (LB), Texas Christian | 1971–72 |
| Clark, Mike (K/E), Texas A&M | 1963 | Creswell, Smiley (DE), Michigan State | 1985 |
| Clark, Myers (B), Ohio State | 1934 | Crews, Terry (LB), Western Michigan | 1996 |
| Clark, Willie (CB), Notre Dame | 1997 | Cronin, Bill (E), Boston College | 1965 |
| Clarke, Adrien (G), Ohio State | 2004 | Cross, Irv (DB), Northwestern | 1961–65, |
| Clarke, Ken (DT), Syracuse | 1978–87 | | 1969 |
| Clayton, Don (T), No College | 1936 | Crowe, Larry (RB), Texas Southern | 1972 |
| Clemons, Topper (RB), Wake Forest† | 1987 | Crutchfield, Darrel (CB), Clemson | 2001 |
| Cobb, Garry (LB), Southern California | 1985–87 | Cuba, Paul (T), Pittsburgh | 1933–35 |
| Cody, Bill (LB), Auburn | 1972 | Culbreath, Jim (FB), Oklahoma | 1980 |
| Colavito, Rocky (LB), Wake Forest | 1975 | Cullars, Willie (DE), Kansas State | 1974 |
| Cole, John (B), St. Joseph's | 1938–40 | Cumby, George (LB), Kentucky† | 1987 |
| Cole, Trent (LB), Cincinnati | 2005 | Cunningham, Dick (LB), Arkansas | 1973 |
| Coleman, Al (DB), Tennessee State | 1972 | Cunningham, Randall (QB), University | |
| Coleman, Marco (DE), Georgia Tech | 2003 |    of Nevada–Las Vegas | 1985–95 |
| Collie, Bruce (G), Texas-Arlington | 1990–91 | Cuppoletti, Bree (G), Oregon | 1939–40 |
| Colman, Wayne (DB), Temple | 1968–69 | Curcio, Mike (LB), Temple | 1981–82 |
| Combs, William (E), Purdue | 1942 | Curtis, Scott (LB), New Hampshire | 1988 |
| Concannon, Jack (QB), Boston College | 1964–66 | | |
| Conjar, Larry (B), Notre Dame | 1968 | **D** | |
| Conlin, Ray (DT), Ohio State† | 1987 | D'Agostino, Frank (G), Auburn | 1956 |
| Conner, Darion (DE), Jackson State | 1996–97 | Darby, Byron (DE/TE), Southern California | 1983–86 |

Darilek, Trey (T/G), University of
Texas–El Paso 2004

Darling, James (LB), Washington State 1997–2000

Darwin, Matt (C), Texas A&M 1986–90

Davis, Al (B), Tennessee State 1971–72

Davis, Antone (T), Tennessee 1991–95

Davis, Bob (B), Kentucky 1942

Davis, Norm (G), Grambling 1970

Davis, Pernell (DT), Alabama-Birmingham 1999–2000

Davis, Stan (WB), Memphis State 1973

Davis, Sylvester (B), Geneva 1933

Davis, Vern (DB), Western Michigan 1971

Dawkins, Brian (FS), Clemson 1996

Dawson, Dale (K), Eastern Kentucky 1988

Dean, Ted (B), Wichita 1960–63

DeLine, Steve (K), Colorado State 1989

Dellenbach, Jeff (G/C), Wisconsin 1999

DeLucca, Jerry (T), Middle Tennessee State 1959

Demas, George (G), Washington &
Jefferson College 1933

Dempsey, Jack (T), Bucknell 1934, 1937

Dempsey, Tom (K), Palomar Junior College 1971–74

Dennard, Mark (C), Texas A&M 1984–85

Dent, Richard (DE), Tennessee State 1997

DeSantis, Dan (B), Niagara 1941

Detmer, Koy (QB), Colorado 1997

Detmer, Ty (QB), Brigham Young University 1996–97

DeVaughn, Dennis (DB), Bishop 1982–83

Dial, Alan (DB), UCLA 1989

Dial, Benjy (B), Eastern New Mexico 1967

Diaz-Infante, David (G), San Jose State 1999

Dickerson, Kori (TE), Southern California 2003

DiFlippo, Dave (G), Villanova 1941

Dimmick, Tom (T), Houston 1956

Dimry, Charles (CB), University of
Nevada–Las Vegas 1997

Dingle, Nate (LB), Cincinnati 1995

DiRenzo, Danny (P), No College 1948

Dirks, Mike (G), Wyoming 1968–71

Disend, Leo (T), Albright 1943

Ditka, Mike (E), Pittsburgh 1967–68

Dixon, Al (TE), Iowa State 1983

Dixon, Floyd (WR), Stephen F. Austin 1992

Dixon, Ronnie (DT), Cincinnati 1995–96

Dixon, Zachary (RB), Temple 1980

Dobbins, Herb (T), San Diego State 1974

Dogins, Kevin (G/C), Texas A&M–Kingsville 2003

Dorow, Al (B), Michigan State 1957

Dorsey, Dean (K), Toronto 1988

Doss, Noble (B), Texas 1947–48

Douglas, Dameane (WR), California 1999–2002

Douglas, Hugh (LB/DE), Central
State (Ohio) 2002, 2004

Douglas, Merrill (B), Utah 1962

Douglas, Otis (T), W & W. 1946–49

Dow, Elwood (B), West Texas State 1938–40

Dowda, Harry (B), Wake Forest 1954–55

Doyle, Ted (T), Nebraska 1943

Drake, Joe (DT), Arizona 1985

Drake, Troy (T), Indiana 1995–97

Drummond, Robert (RB), Syracuse 1989–91

Duckworth, Bobby (WR), Arkansas 1986

Dudley, Paul (B), Arkansas 1963

Dumbauld, John (DE), Kentucky 1987–88

Duncan, Rick (K), Eastern Montana State 1968

Dunek, Ken (TE), Memphis State 1980

Dunn, Jason (TE), Eastern Kentucky 1996–98

Dunstan, Bill (DT), Utah State 1973–76

Durko, John (E), Albright 1944

**E**

Edwards, Anthony (WR), New Mexico
Highlands 1989–90

Edwards, Herman (DB), San Diego State 1977–85

Ehlers, Tom (LB), Kentucky 1975–77

Eibner, John (T), Kentucky 1941–42, 1946

Eiden, Edmund (B), Scranton 1944

Elewonibi, Moe (T), Brigham Young
University 1995

Ellis, Drew (T), Texas Christian University 1938–40

Ellis, Ray (S), Ohio State 1981–85

Ellstrom, Marvin (B), Oklahoma City 1934

Emanuel, Charles (S), West Virginia 1997

Emelianchik, Pete (E), Richmond 1967

| | | |
|---|---|---|
| Emmons, Carlos (LB), Arkansas State | 2000–03 | |
| Emmons, Franklin (B), Oregon | 1940 | |
| Ena, Justin (LB), Brigham Young University | 2002–03, 2005 | |
| Engles, Rick (P), Tulsa | 1978 | |
| Enke, Fred (B), Arizona | 1952 | |
| Ephraim, Alonzo (C), Alabama | 2003–04 | |
| Erdlitz, Richard (B), Northwestern | 1942, 1945 | |
| Estes, Larry (DE), Alcorn A&M | 1972 | |
| Evans, Byron (LB), Arizona | 1987–94 | |
| Evans, Donald (DE), Winston Salem State | 1988 | |
| Evans, Mike (C), Boston College | 1968–73 | |
| Everett, Eric (CB), Texas Tech | 1988–89 | |
| Everett, Major (FB), Mississippi College | 1983–85 | |
| Everitt, Steve (C), Michigan | 1997–99 | |

**F**

| | |
|---|---|
| Fagioli, Carl (G), No College | 1944 |
| Farmer, Ray (LB), Duke | 1996–98 |
| Farragut, Ken (C), Mississippi | 1951–54 |
| Fazio, Ron (TE), Maryland† | 1987 |
| Feagles, Jeff (P), Miami (Florida) | 1990–93 |
| Feather, E.E. (B), Kansas State | 1933 |
| Feehery, Gerry (C/G), Syracuse | 1983–87 |
| Feeley, A.J. (QB), Oregon | 2001–03 |
| Felber, Fred (E), North Dakota | 1933 |
| Feller, Happy (K), Texas | 1971 |
| Fencl, Richard (E), Northwestern | 1933 |
| Ferko, John (G), West Chester | 1937–38 |
| Ferrante, Jack (E), No College | 1941, 1944–50 |
| Ferrara, Frank (DE), Rhode Island | 2003 |
| Ferris, Neil (B), Loyola (California) | 1952 |
| Fiedler, Bill (G), Pennsylvania | 1938 |
| Fiedler, Jay (QB), Dartmouth | 1994–95 |
| Field, Richard (G), No College | 1939–40 |
| Finn, Mike (T), Arkansas–Pine Bluff | 1994 |
| Finneran, Brian (WR), Villanova | 1999 |
| Fitzgerald, Mickey (FB), Virginia Tech | 1981 |
| Fitzkee, Scott (WR), Penn State | 1979–80 |
| Flanigan, Jim (DT), Notre Dame | 2003 |
| Flores, Mike (DT), Louisville | 1991–94 |
| Floyd, Eric (G), Auburn | 1992–93 |

| | |
|---|---|
| Fogle, DeShawn (LB), Kansas State | 1997 |
| Folsom, Steve (TE), Utah | 1981 |
| Fontenot, Chris (TE), McNeese State | 1998 |
| Ford, Charles (DB), Houston | 1974 |
| Ford, Fredric (CB), Mississippi Valley State | 1997 |
| Foules, Elbert (CB), Alcorn State | 1983–87 |
| Fox, Terry (B), Miami (Florida) | 1941, 1945 |
| Frahm, Herald (B), Nebraska | 1935 |
| Fraley, Hank (C/G), Robert Morris | 2000 |
| France, Todd (K), Toledo | 2005 |
| Frank, Joseph (T), Georgetown | 1941, 1943 |
| Franklin, Cleveland (RB), Baylor | 1977–78 |
| Franklin, Tony (K), Texas A&M | 1979–83 |
| Franks, Dennis (C), Michigan | 1976–78 |
| Frazier, Derrick (CB), Texas A&M | 1993–95 |
| Freeman, Antonio (WR), Virginia Tech | 2002 |
| Freeman, Bob (B), Auburn | 1960–61 |
| Frey, Glenn (B), Temple | 1936–37 |
| Friedlund, Bob (E), Michigan State | 1946 |
| Friedman, Bob (G), Washington | 1944 |
| Fritts, George (T), Clemson | 1945 |
| Fritz, Ralph (G), Michigan | 1941 |
| Fritzsche, Jim (T/G), Purdue | 1983 |
| Frizzell, William (S), North Carolina Central | 1986–90, 1992–93 |
| Fryar, Irving (WR), Nebraska | 1996–98 |
| Fuller, Frank (T), Kentucky | 1963 |
| Fuller, James (S), Portland State | 1996 |
| Fuller, William (DE), North Carolina | 1994–96 |
| Furio, Dominic (C), University of Nevada–Las Vegas | 2004 |

**G**

| | |
|---|---|
| Gabbard, Steve (OT), Florida State | 1989 |
| Gabriel, Roman (B), North Carolina State | 1973–77 |
| Gambold, Bob (B), Washington State | 1953 |
| Gaona, Bob (T), Wake Forest | 1957 |
| Gardner, Barry (LB), Northwestern | 1999–2002 |
| Garner, Charlie (RB), Tennessee | 1994–98 |
| Garrity, Gregg (WR), Penn State | 1984–89 |
| Gary, Russell (DB), Nebraska | 1986 |
| Gauer, Charles (E), Colgate | 1943–45 |

| | | | |
|---|---|---|---|
| Gay, Blenda (DE), Fayetteville State | 1975–76 | Graham, Tom (G), Temple | 1935 |
| George, Ed (T), Wake Forest | 1976–78 | Grant, Bud (E), Minnesota | 1951–52 |
| George, Raymond (T), Southern California | 1940 | Grant, Otis (WR), Michigan State† | 1987 |
| Gerber, Elwood (G), Alabama | 1941–42 | Grasmanis, Paul (DT), Notre Dame | 2000 |
| Gerhard, Chris (FS), East Stroudsburg† | 1987 | Graves, Ray (C), Tennessee | 1942–43, 1946 |
| Gerhart, Tom (DB), Ohio University | 1992 | Gray, Cecil (G/DT), North Carolina | 1990–91 |
| Gersbach, Carl (LB), West Chester | 1970 | Gray, Jim (B), Toledo | 1967 |
| Ghecas, Lou (B), Georgetown | 1941 | Gray, Mel (KR/RB), Purdue | 1997 |
| Giammona, Louie (RB), Utah State | 1978–82 | Green, Donnie (T), Purdue | 1977 |
| Giancanelli, Hal (B), Loyola (California) | 1953–56 | Green, Jamaal (DE), Miami (Florida) | 2003–04 |
| Giannelli, Mario (G), Boston College | 1948–51 | Green, John (E), Tulsa | 1947–51 |
| Gibbs, Pat (DB), Lamar | 1972 | Green, Roy (WR), Henderson State | 1991–92 |
| Gibron, Abe (G), Purdue | 1956–57 | Gregg, Kelly (DT), Oklahoma | 1999–2000 |
| Giddens, Frank (T), New Mexico | 1981–82 | Gregory, Ken (E), Whittier | 1962 |
| Giddens, Herschel (T), Louisiana Tech | 1938 | Griffin, Don (CB), Middle Tennessee State | 1996 |
| Gilbert, Lewis (TE), Florida | 1980 | Griffin, Jeff (CB), Utah† | 1987 |
| Giles, Jimmie (TE), Alcorn State | 1987–89 | Griggs, Anthony (LB), Ohio State | 1982–85 |
| Gill, Roger (B), Texas Tech | 1964–65 | Grooms, Elois (DE), Tennessee Tech† | 1987 |
| Gilmore, Jim (T), Ohio State | 1986 | Gros, Earl (B), Louisiana State University | 1964–66 |
| Ginney, Jerry (G), Santa Clara | 1940 | Grossman, Burt (DE), Pittsburgh | 1994 |
| Glass, Glenn (B), Tennessee | 1964–65 | Gudd, Leonard (E), Temple | 1934 |
| Gloden, Fred (B), Tulane | 1941 | Gude, Henry (G), Vanderbilt | 1946 |
| Glover, Rich (DT), Nebraska | 1975 | Guglielmi, Ralph (QB), Notre Dame | 1963 |
| Goebel, Brad (QB), Baylor | 1991 | Guillory, Tony (LB), Lamar Tech | 1969 |
| Golden, Tim (LB), Florida | 1985 | Gunn, Mark (DL), Pittsburgh | 1995–96 |
| Goldston, Ralph (B), Youngstown State | 1952, 1954–55 | Gunnels, Riley (T), Georgia | 1960–64 |
| Golic, Mike (DT), Notre Dame | 1987–92 | **H** | |
| Gollomb, Rudy (G), Carroll (Wisconsin) | 1936 | Hackney, Elmer (B), Kansas State | 1940–41 |
| Gonya, Robert (T), Northwestern | 1933–34 | Haddix, Michael (FB), Mississippi State | 1983–88 |
| Goode, John (TE), Youngstown State | 1985 | Haden, Nick (G), Penn State | 1986 |
| Goode, Rob (B), Texas A&M | 1955 | Hager, Britt (LB), Texas | 1989–94 |
| Goodwin, Marvin (FS), UCLA | 1994 | Hairston, Carl (DE), Maryland Eastern Shore | 1976–83 |
| Goodwin, Ron (E), Baylor | 1963–68 | Hajek, Charles (C), Northwestern | 1934 |
| Gordon, Lamar (RB), North Dakota State | 2005 | Hall, Andy (QB), Delaware | 2005 |
| Gorecki, Chuck (LB), Boston College† | 1987 | Hall, Irving (B), Brown | 1942 |
| Gossage, Gene (E), Northwestern | 1960–62 | Hall, Rhett (DT), California | 1995–98 |
| Gouveia, Kurt (LB), Brigham Young University | 1995 | Hallstrom, Ron (G), Iowa | 1993 |
| Graham, Dave (T), Virginia | 1963–69 | Halverson, Bill (T), Oregon State | 1942 |
| Graham, Jeff (WR), Ohio State | 1998 | Halverson, Dean (LB), Washington | 1973–76 |
| Graham, Lyle (C), Richmond | 1941 | Hamilton, Ray (E), Arkansas | 1940 |

| | |
|---|---|
| Hamilton, Skip (DT), Southern† | 1987 |
| Hamiter, Uhuru (DE), Delaware State | 2000–01 |
| Hamner, Thomas (RB), Minnesota | 2000 |
| Hampton, Dave (RB), Wyoming | 1976 |
| Hampton, William (CB), Murray State | 2001 |
| Hankton, Karl (WR), Trinity College (Illinois) | 1998 |
| Hansen, Roscoe (T), North Carolina | 1951 |
| Hanson, Homer (C), Kansas State | 1935 |
| Hanson, Thomas "Swede" (B), Temple | 1933–37 |
| Harding, Greg (DB), Nicholls† | 1987 |
| Harding, Roger (C), California | 1947 |
| Hardy, Andre (RB), St. Mary's (California) | 1984 |
| Hargrove, Marvin (WR), Richmond | 1990 |
| Harmon, Andy (DT), Kent State | 1991–97 |
| Harper, Maurice (C), Austin | 1937–40 |
| Harrington, Perry (RB), Jackson State | 1980–83 |
| Harris, Al (LB), Arizona State | 1989–90 |
| Harris, Al (CB), Texas A&M–Kingsville | 1998–2002 |
| Harris, Jim (B), Oklahoma | 1957 |
| Harris, Jon (DE), Virginia | 1997–98 |
| Harris, Leroy (FB), Arkansas State | 1979–82 |
| Harris, Richard (DE), Grambling | 1971–73 |
| Harris, Rod (WR), Texas A&M | 1990–91 |
| Harris, Tim (DE), Memphis State | 1993 |
| Harrison, Bob (LB), Oklahoma | 1962–63 |
| Harrison, Dennis (DE), Vanderbilt | 1978–84 |
| Harrison, Granville (E), Mississippi State | 1941 |
| Harrison, Tyreo (LB), Notre Dame | 2002–03 |
| Hart, Clinton (S), Central Florida Community College | 2003–04 |
| Hart, Dick (G), No College | 1967–71 |
| Hartman, Fred (T), Rice | 1948 |
| Harvey, Richard (DB), Jackson State | 1970 |
| Haskins, Jon (LB), Stanford | 1998 |
| Hasselbeck, Tim (QB), Boston College | 2002 |
| Hauck, Tim (SS), Montana | 1999–2002 |
| Hawkins, Ben (FL), Arizona State | 1966–73 |
| Hayden, Aaron (RB), Tennessee | 1998 |
| Hayden, Ken (C), Arkansas | 1942 |
| Hayes, Ed (DB), Morgan State | 1970 |
| Hayes, Joe (WR/KR), Central State (Oklahoma) | 1984 |
| Haymond, Alvin (B), Southern University | 1968 |
| Heath, Jo Jo (DB), Pittsburgh | 1981 |
| Hebron, Vaughn (RB), Virginia Tech | 1993–95 |
| Heck, Ralph (LB), Colorado | 1963–65 |
| Hegamin, George (G/T), North Carolina State | 1998 |
| Heller, Ron (T), Penn State | 1988–92 |
| Henderson, Jerome (CB), Clemson | 1995 |
| Henderson, Zac (S), Oklahoma | 1980 |
| Hendrickson, Steve (LB), California | 1995 |
| Henry, Maurice (LB), Kansas State | 1990 |
| Henry, Wally (WR), UCLA | 1977–82 |
| Henson, Gary (E), Colorado | 1963 |
| Herremans, Todd (T), Saginaw Valley State | 2005 |
| Herrod, Jeff (LB), Mississippi | 1997 |
| Hershey, Kirk (E), Cornell | 1941 |
| Hertel, Rob (QB), Southern California | 1980 |
| Hewitt, Bill (E), Michigan | 1936–39, 1943 |
| Hicks, Artis (T), Memphis | 2002 |
| Higgins, Tom (T), North Carolina | 1954–55 |
| Higgs, Mark (RB), Kentucky | 1989 |
| Hill, Fred (E), Southern California | 1965–71 |
| Hill, King (B), Rice | 1961–68 |
| Hinkle, Jack (B), Syracuse | 1941–47 |
| Hix, Billy (E), Arkansas | 1950 |
| Hoage, Terry (S), Georgia | 1986–90 |
| Hoague, Joe (B), Colgate | 1943 |
| Hobbs, Bill (LB), Texas A&M | 1969–71 |
| Hodges, Reggie (P), Ball State | 2005 |
| Hogan, Mike (FB), University of Tennessee–Chattanooga | 1976–78, 1980 |
| Holcomb, William (T), Texas Tech | 1937 |
| Holly, Bob (QB), Princeton | 1984 |
| Holmes, Lester (G), Jackson State | 1993–96 |
| Hood, Roderick (CB), Auburn | 2003 |
| Hooks, Alvin (WR), California-Northridge | 1981 |
| Hoover, Mel (WR), Arizona State | 1982–84 |
| Hopkins, Wes (FS), Southern Methodist University | 1983–93 |
| Horan, Mike (P), Long Beach State | 1984–85 |
| Hord, Roy (G), Duke | 1962 |
| Horn, Marty (QB), Lehigh† | 1987 |
| Horrell, Bill (G), Michigan State | 1952 |

| | | | |
|---|---|---|---|
| Hoss, Clark (TE), Oregon | 1972 | Jackson, Randy (RB), Wichita State | 1974 |
| Howard, Bob (CB), San Diego State | 1978–79 | Jackson, Trenton (FL), Illinois | 1966 |
| Howell, Lane (T), Grambling | 1965–69 | Jacobs, David (K), Syracuse† | 1987 |
| Hoyem, Lynn (G), Long Beach State | 1964–67 | Jacobs, Proverb (T), California | 1958 |
| Hoying, Bobby (QB), Ohio State | 1996–98 | James, Angelo (CB), Sacramento State† | 1987 |
| Hrabetin, Frank (T), Loyola (California) | 1942 | James, Ronald "Po" (RB), New Mexico State | 1972–75 |
| Huarte, John (QB), Notre Dame | 1968 | Janet, Ernie (T), Washington | 1975 |
| Hudson, Bob (B), Clemson | 1953–55, | Jarmoluk, Mike (T), Temple | 1949–55 |
| | 1957–58 | Jarvi, Toimi (B), Northern Illinois | 1944 |
| Hudson, John (G), Auburn | 1991–95 | Jasper, Edward (DT), Texas A&M | 1997–98 |
| Hughes, Chuck (FL), Texas El Paso | 1967–69 | Jaworski, Ron (QB), Youngstown State | 1977–86 |
| Hughes, William (C), Texas | 1937–40 | Jefferson, Greg (DE), Central Florida | 1995–2000 |
| Hultz, Don (DT), University of South | | Jefferson, William (B), Mississippi State | 1942 |
| Mississippi | 1964–73 | Jelesky, Tom (T), Purdue | 1985–86 |
| Humbert, Dick (E), Richmond | 1941, 1945–49 | Jells, Dietrich (WR), Pittsburgh | 1998–99 |
| Humphrey, Claude (DE), Tennessee State | 1979–81 | Jenkins, Izel (CB), North Carolina State | 1988–92 |
| Hunt, Calvin (C), Baylor | 1970 | Jeter, Tommy (DT), Texas | 1992–95 |
| Hunter, Herman (RB/KR), Tennessee State | 1985 | Jiles, Dwayne (LB), Texas Tech | 1985–89 |
| Huth, Gerry (G), Wake Forest | 1959–60 | Johansson, Ove (K), Abilene Christian | 1977 |
| Hutton, Tom (P), Tennessee | 1995–98 | Johnson, Albert (B), Kentucky | 1942 |
| Huxhold, Ken (G), Wisconsin | 1954–58 | Johnson, Alonzo (LB), Florida | 1986–87 |
| Huzvar, John (B), North Carolina State | 1952 | Johnson, Alvin (B), Hardin-Simmons | 1948 |
| | | Johnson, Bill (DT), Michigan State | 1998–99 |
| **I** | | Johnson, Charles (WR), Colorado | 1999–2000 |
| | | Johnson, Charlie (MG), Colorado | 1977–81 |
| Ignatius, James (G), Holy Cross | 1935 | Johnson, Chris (DB), Millersville† | 1987 |
| Illman, Ed (B), Montana University | 1933 | Johnson, Dirk (P), Northern Colorado | 2003 |
| Ingram, Mark (WR), Michigan State | 1996 | Johnson, Don (B), California | 1953–55 |
| Irvin, Willie (B), Florida A&M | 1953 | Johnson, Dwight (DE), Baylor | 2000 |
| | | Johnson, Eric (DB), Washington State | 1977–78 |
| **J** | | Johnson, Gene (B), Cincinnati | 1959–60 |
| | | Johnson, Jay (LB), East Texas State | 1969 |
| Jackson, Al (CB), Georgia | 1994 | Johnson, Jimmie (TE), Howard | 1995–98 |
| Jackson, Bob (B), Alabama | 1960 | Johnson, Kevin (DT), Texas Southern | 1995–96 |
| Jackson, Don (B), North Carolina | 1936 | Johnson, Lee (P), Brigham Young University | 2002 |
| Jackson, Earnest (RB), Texas A&M | 1985–86 | Johnson, Maurice (TE), Temple | 1991–94 |
| Jackson, Greg (FS), Louisiana State | | Johnson, Norm (K), UCLA | 1999 |
| University | 1994–95 | Johnson, Reggie (TE), Florida State | 1995 |
| Jackson, Harold (WR), Jackson State | 1969–72 | Johnson, Ron (DE), Shippensburg | 2003 |
| Jackson, Jamaal (G/C), Delaware State | 2003 | Johnson, Ron (WR), Long Beach State | 1985–89 |
| Jackson, Johnny (DE), Southern | 1977 | Johnson, Vaughan (LB), North Carolina | |
| Jackson, Keith (TE), Oklahoma | 1988–91 | State | 1994 |
| Jackson, Kenny (WR), Penn State | 1984–88, | | |
| | 1990–91 | | |

| | |
|---|---|
| Jonas, Don (B), Penn State | 1962 |
| Jones, Chris T. (WR), Miami (Florida) | 1995–97 |
| Jones, Dhani (LB), Michigan | 2004–05 |
| Jones, Don (B), Washington | 1940 |
| Jones, Harry (B), Arkansas | 1967–71 |
| Jones, Jimmie (DT/DE), Miami (Florida) | 1997 |
| Jones, Joe (DE), Tennessee State | 1974–75 |
| Jones, Julian (S), Missouri | 2001–02 |
| Jones, Preston (QB), Georgia | 1993 |
| Jones, Ray (DB), Southern University | 1970 |
| Jones, Spike (P), Georgia | 1975–77 |
| Jones, Tyrone (DB), Arkansas State | 1989 |
| Jordan, Andrew (TE), Western Carolina | 1998 |
| Jorgenson, Carl (T), St. Mary's | 1935 |
| Joseph, James (RB), Auburn | 1991–94 |
| Joyner, Seth (LB), Texas–El Paso | 1986–93 |
| Jurgensen, Sonny (QB), Duke | 1957–63 |

**K**

| | |
|---|---|
| Kab, Vyto (TE), Penn State | 1982–85 |
| Kalu, N.D. (DE), Rice | 1997, 2001 |
| Kane, Carl (B), St. Louis | 1936 |
| Kapele, John (T), Brigham Young University | 1962 |
| Kaplan, Bennie (G), West Maryland | 1942 |
| Karnofsky, Sonny (B), Arizona | 1945 |
| Kasky, Ed (T), Villanova | 1942 |
| Kaufusi, Steve (DE), Brigham Young University | 1989–90 |
| Kavel, George (B), Carnegie Tech | 1934 |
| Kearse, Jevon (DE), Florida | 2004 |
| Keeling, Ray (T), Texas | 1938–39 |
| Keen, Allen (B), Arkansas | 1937–38 |
| Kekeris, Jim (T), Missouri | 1947 |
| Keller, Ken (B), North Carolina | 1956–57 |
| Kelley, Bob (C), West Texas State | 1955–56 |
| Kelley, Dwight (LB), Ohio State | 1966–72 |
| Kelly, Jim (E), Notre Dame | 1965–67 |
| Kelly, Joe (LB), Washington | 1996 |
| Kemp, Jeff (QB), Dartmouth | 1991 |
| Kenneally, George (E), St. Bonaventure | 1933–35 |
| Kenney, Steve (G), Clemson | 1980–85 |
| Kersey, Merritt (P), West Chester | 1974–75 |

| | |
|---|---|
| Key, Wade (G/T), Southwest Texas State | 1970–80 |
| Keyes, Leroy (DB), Purdue | 1969–72 |
| Keys, Howard (T/C), Oklahoma State | 1960–64 |
| Khayat, Ed (T), Tulane | 1958–61, 1964–65 |
| Kilroy, Frank (T), Temple | 1943–55 |
| Kimmel, Jon (LB), Colgate | 1985 |
| Kinder, Randy (CB), Notre Dame | 1997 |
| King, Don (T), Kentucky | 1956 |
| Kirchbaum, Kelly (LB), Kentucky† | 1987 |
| Kirkland, Levon (LB), Clemson | 2002 |
| Kirkman, Roger (B), Washington & Jefferson | 1933–35 |
| Kirksey, Roy (G), Maryland Eastern Shore | 1973–74 |
| Kish, Ben (B), Pittsburgh | 1942–49 |
| Klingel, John (DE), Eastern Kentucky | 1987–88 |
| Klopenburg, Harry (T), Fordham | 1936 |
| Kmetovic, Pete (B), Stanford | 1946 |
| Knapper, Joe (B), Ottawa University (Kansas) | 1934 |
| Knox, Charles (T), St. Edmonds | 1937 |
| Koeninger, Art (C), Chattanooga | 1933 |
| Kolberg, Elmer (B), Oregon State | 1939–40 |
| Koman, Bill (LB), North Carolina | 1957–58 |
| Konecny, Mark (RB/PR), Alma | 1988 |
| Konopka, John (B), Temple | 1936 |
| Kostos, Anthony (E), Bucknell | 1933 |
| Kowalczyk, Walt (B), Michigan State | 1958–59 |
| Kowalkowski, Scott (LB), Notre Dame | 1991–93 |
| Kramer, Kent (E), Minnesota | 1971–74 |
| Kraynak, Rich (LB), Pittsburgh | 1983–86 |
| Krepfle, Keith (TE), Iowa State | 1975–81 |
| Kresky, Joseph (G), Wisconsin | 1933–35 |
| Krieger, Robert (E), Dartmouth | 1941, 1946 |
| Kriel, Emmet (G), Baylor | 1939 |
| Kuczynski, Bert (E), Pennsylvania | 1946 |
| Kullman, Mike (SS), Kutztown State† | 1987 |
| Kupcinet, Irv (B), North Dakota | 1935 |
| Kusko, John (B), Temple | 1936–38 |

**L**

| | |
|---|---|
| Laack, Galen (G), College of the Pacific | 1958 |
| Labinjo, Mike (LB), Michigan State | 2004 |
| Lachman, Dick (B), No College | 1933–35 |

Lainhart, Porter (B), Washington State — 1933

Landeta, Sean (P), Towson State — 1999–2002, 2005

Landsberg, Mort (B), Cornell — 1941

Landsee, Bob (G/C), Wisconsin — 1986–87

Lang, Israel (B), Tennessee State — 1964–68

Lankas, James (B), St. Mary's (Texas) — 1942

Lansford, Buck (T), Texas — 1955–57

Lapham, Bill (C), Iowa — 1960

Larson, Bill (TE), Colorado State — 1978

Latimer, Al (CB), Clemson — 1979

Laux, Ted (B), St. Joseph's — 1942–44

Lavender, Joe (DB), San Diego State — 1973–75

Lavergne, Damian (T), Louisiana Tech — 2003

Lavette, Robert (RB/KR), Georgia Tech — 1987

Lawrence, Kent (WR), Georgia — 1969

Lawrence, Reggie (WR), North Carolina State — 1993

Lazetich, Pete (DT), Stanford — 1976–77

Le Bel, Harper (TE), Colorado State — 1990

Leathers, Milton (G), Georgia — 1933

Lechthaler, Roy (G), Lebanon Valley — 1933

Ledbetter, Toy (B), Oklahoma A&M — 1950, 1953–55

Lee, Amp (RB), Florida State — 2000

Lee, Bernie (B), Villanova — 1938

Lee, Byron (LB), Ohio State† — 1986–87

Leggett, Scott (G), Central State (Ohio)† — 1987

LeJeune, Norman (S), Louisiana State
University — 2003

LeMaster, Frank (LB), Kentucky — 1974–83

Leonard, Jim (B), Notre Dame — 1934–37

Leshinski, Ron (TE), Army — 1999

Levanites, Stephen (T), Boston College — 1942

Levens, Dorsey (RB), Georgia Tech — 2002, 2004

Lewis, Chad (TE), Brigham Young
University — 1997–2004

Lewis, Greg (WR), Illinois — 2003

Lewis, Joe (T), Compton — 1962

Lewis, Michael (S), Colorado — 2002

Leyendecker, Charles "Tex" (T), Vanderbilt — 1933

Lilly, Sammy (DB), Georgia Tech — 1989–90

Lince, Dave (E), North Dakota — 1966–67

Lindskog, Vic (C), Stanford — 1944–51

Lio, Augie (G), Georgetown — 1946

Lipski, John "Bull" (C), Temple — 1933–34

Liske, Pete (QB), Penn State — 1971–72

Liter, Greg (DE), Iowa† — 1987

Little, Dave (TE), Middle Tennessee State — 1985–89

Lloyd, Dave (LB/K), Georgia — 1963–70

Lofton, James (WR), Stanford — 1993

Logan, Randy (S), Michigan — 1973–83

Long, Matt (C), San Diego State† — 1987

Looney, Don (E), Texas Christian University — 1940

Lou, Ron (C), Arizona State — 1975

Louderback, Tom (LB), San Jose State — 1958–59

Love, Clarence (CB), Toledo — 1998

Love, Sean (G), Penn State — 1997

Lucas, Dick (E), Boston College — 1960–63

Lueck, Bill (G), Arizona — 1975

Luft, Don (E), Indiana — 1954

Luken, Tom (G), Purdue — 1972–78

Lusk, Herb (RB), Long Beach State — 1976–78

## M

MacAfee, Ken (E), Alabama — 1959

MacDowell, Jay (E), Washington — 1946–51

Macioszczyk, Art (B), Western Michigan — 1944–47

Mack, Bill (FL), Notre Dame — 1964

Mackey, Kyle (QB), East Texas State — 1986

Mackrides, Bill (B), Nevada — 1947–51

MacMurdo, Jim (T), Pittsburgh — 1934–37

Magee, John (G), Rice — 1948–55

Mahalic, Drew (LB), Notre Dame — 1976–78

Mahe, Reno (RB/KR), Brigham Young
University — 2003

Mallory, John (B), West Virginia — 1968

Malone, Art (RB), Arizona State — 1975–76

Mamula, Mike (DE), Boston College — 1995–2000

Mandarino, Mike (G), LaSalle — 1944–45

Manning, Roosevelt (DT), Northeastern
Oklahoma — 1975

Mansfield, Ray (C), Washington — 1963

Mansfield, Von (DB), Wisconsin — 1982

Manske, Ed (E), Northwestern — 1935–36

Manton, Taldon (B), Texas Christian
University — 1940

| | |
|---|---|
| Manzini, Baptiste (C), St. Vincent's | 1944–45, 1948 |
| Marchi, Basilio (C), New York University | 1941–42 |
| Marcus, Alex (E), Temple | 1933 |
| Mark, Greg (DE), Miami (Florida) | 1990 |
| Maronic, Duke (G), No College | 1944–50 |
| Marshall, Anthony (SS), Louisiana State University | 1998 |
| Marshall, Keyonta (DT), Grand Valley State | 2005 |
| Marshall, Larry (KR), Maryland | 1974–77 |
| Marshall, Whit (LB), Georgia | 1996 |
| Martin, Aaron (DB), North Carolina College | 1966–67 |
| Martin, Cecil (FB), Wisconsin | 1999–2002 |
| Martin, Kelvin (WR), Boston College | 1995 |
| Martin, Steve (DT), Missouri | 1998–99 |
| Mass, Wayne (T), Clemson | 1972 |
| Masters, Bob (B), Baylor | 1937–38, 1941–43 |
| Masters, Walt (B), Pennsylvania | 1936 |
| Matesic, Ed (B), Pittsburgh | 1934–35 |
| Matson, Ollie (B), San Francisco | 1964–66 |
| Mavraides, Menil (G), Notre Dame | 1954, 1957 |
| May, Dean (QB), Louisville | 1984 |
| Mayberry, Jermane (G/T), Texas A&M–Kingsville | 1996–2004 |
| Mayes, Rufus (T), Ohio State | 1979 |
| Maynard, Les (B), Rider | 1933 |
| Mazzanti, Jerry (E), Arkansas | 1963 |
| McAfee, Wesley (B), Duke | 1941 |
| McAlister, James (RB), UCLA | 1975–76 |
| McCants, Darnerien (WR), Delaware State | 2005 |
| McChesney, Bob (E), Hardin-Simmons | 1950 |
| McClellan, Mike (B), Oklahoma | 1962–63 |
| McCloskey, Mike (TE), Penn State | 1987 |
| McCoo, Eric (RB), Penn State | 2004 |
| McCoy, Matt (LB), San Diego State | 2005 |
| McCrary, Fred (FB), Mississippi State | 1995 |
| McCullough, Hugh (B), Oklahoma | 1943 |
| McCusker, Jim (T), Pittsburgh | 1959–62 |
| McDonald, Don (E), Oklahoma | 1944–45 |
| McDonald, Lester (E), Nebraska | 1940 |
| McDonald, Tommy (FL), Oklahoma | 1957–63 |
| McDonough, Robert (G), Duke | 1942–46 |

| | |
|---|---|
| McDougle, Jerome (DE), Miami (Florida) | 2003–04 |
| McFadden, Paul (K), Youngstown State | 1984–87 |
| McHale, Tom (G/T), Cornell | 1993–94 |
| McHugh, Pat (B), Georgia Tech | 1947–51 |
| McIntyre, Guy (G), Georgia | 1995–96 |
| McKeever, Marlin (LB), Southern California | 1973 |
| McKenzie, Kevin (WR), Washington State | 1998 |
| McKenzie, Raleigh (C), Tennessee | 1995–96 |
| McKnight, Dennis (G), Drake | 1991 |
| McMahon, Jim (QB), Brigham Young University | 1990–92 |
| McMahon, Mike (QB), Rutgers | 2005 |
| McMillan, Erik (S), Missouri | 1993 |
| McMillen, Dan (DE), Colorado† | 1987 |
| McMillian, Mark (DB), Alabama | 1992–95 |
| McMullen, Billy (WR), Virginia | 2003 |
| McNabb, Dexter (FB), Florida | 1995 |
| McNabb, Donovan (QB), Syracuse | 1999 |
| McNeill, Tom (P), Stephen F. Austin | 1971–73 |
| McPherson, Don (QB), Syracuse | 1988–90 |
| McPherson, Forest (T), Nebraska | 1935–37 |
| McRae, Jerrold (WR), Tennessee State | 1979 |
| McTyer, Tim (CB), Brigham Young University | 1997–98 |
| Meadows, Ed (E), Duke | 1958 |
| Medved, Ron (DB), Washington | 1966–70 |
| Mellekas, John (T), Arizona | 1963 |
| Mercer, Giradie (DT), Marshall | 2000 |
| Merkens, Guido (QB), Sam Houston State† | 1987 |
| Meyer, Fred (E), Stanford | 1942, 1945 |
| Meyers, John (T), Washington | 1964–67 |
| Miano, Rich (DB), Hawaii | 1991–94 |
| Michaels, Ed (G), Villanova | 1943–46 |
| Michel, Mike (P/K), Stanford | 1978 |
| Michels, John (T), Southern California | 1999 |
| Michels, John (G), Tennessee | 1953 |
| Middlebrook, Oren (WR), Arkansas State | 1978 |
| Mike-Mayer, Nick (K), Temple | 1977–78 |
| Mikell, Quintin (S), Boise State | 2003 |
| Millard, Keith (DT), Washington State | 1993 |
| Miller, Bubba (C/G), Tennessee | 1996–01 |

| | |
|---|---|
| Miller, Don (B), Southern Methodist University | 1954 |
| Miller, Tom (E), Hampden-Sydney | 1942–44 |
| Milling, Al (G), Richmond | 1942 |
| Milon, Barnes (G), Austin | 1934 |
| Milons, Freddie (WR), Alabama | 2002 |
| Mira, George (QB), Miami (Florida) | 1969 |
| Miraldi, Dean (T), Utah | 1982–84 |
| Mitcham, Gene (E), Arizona State | 1958 |
| Mitchell, Brian (RB/KR), Southwest University (Louisiana) | 2000–02 |
| Mitchell, Freddie (WR), UCLA | 2001–04 |
| Mitchell, Leonard (DE/T), Houston | 1981–86 |
| Mitchell, Martin (DB), Tulane | 1977 |
| Mitchell, Randall (NT), University of Tennessee–Chattanooga† | 1987 |
| Moats, Ryan (RB), Louisiana State | 2005 |
| Molden, Frank (T), Jackson State | 1968 |
| Monk, Art (WR), Syracuse | 1995 |
| Monroe, Henry (CB), Mississippi State | 1979 |
| Montgomery, Monty (CB), Houston | 2001 |
| Montgomery, Wilbert (RB), Abilene Christian | 1977–84 |
| Mooney, Tim (DE), Western Kentucky† | 1987 |
| Moore, Damon (SS), Ohio State | 1999–2001 |
| Moreno, Zeke (LB), Southern California | 2005 |
| Morey, Sean (WR), Brown | 2001, 2003 |
| Morgan, Dennis (KR), Western Illinois | 1975 |
| Morgan, Mike (LB), Louisiana State University | 1964–67 |
| Morris, Dwaine (DT), Southwest University (Louisiana) | 1985 |
| Morriss, Guy (C), Texas Christian University | 1973–83 |
| Morse, Bobby (RB/KR), Michigan State | 1987 |
| Mortell, Emmett (B), Wisconsin | 1937–39 |
| Moseley, Mark (K), Stephen F. Austin | 1970 |
| Moselle, Dom (B), Superior State (Wisconsin) | 1954 |
| Mrkonic, George (T), Kansas | 1953 |
| Muha, Joe (B), Virginia Military Institute | 1946–50 |
| Muhlmann, Horst (K), No College | 1975–77 |
| Mulligan, George (E), Catholic University | 1936 |
| Murley, Dick (T), Purdue | 1956 |
| Murphy, Nick (P), Arizona State | 2005 |
| Murray, Calvin (HB), Ohio State | 1981–82 |
| Murray, Eddie (K), Tulane | 1994 |
| Murray, Francis (B), Penn | 1939–40 |
| Myers, Brad (B), Bucknell | 1958 |
| Myers, Jack (B), UCLA | 1948–50 |

**N**

| | |
|---|---|
| Nacrelli, Andy (E), Fordham | 1958 |
| Nease, Mike (C/T), University of Tennessee–Chattanooga† | 1987 |
| Nelson, Al (DB), Cincinnati | 1965–73 |
| Nelson, Dennis (T), Illinois State | 1976–77 |
| Nettles, Jim (DB), Wisconsin | 1965–68 |
| Newton, Charles (B), Washington | 1939–40 |
| Nichols, Gerald (DT), Florida State | 1993 |
| Niland, John (G), Iowa | 1975–76 |
| Nipp, Maurice (G), Loyola (California) | 1952–53, 1956 |
| Nocera, John (LB), Iowa | 1959–62 |
| Norby, Jack (B), Idaho | 1934 |
| Nordquist, Mark (G), Pacific | 1968–74 |
| Norton, Jerry (B), Southern Methodist University | 1954–58 |
| Norton, Jim (T), Washington | 1968 |
| Nowak, Walt (E), Villanova | 1944 |

**O**

| | |
|---|---|
| Oakes, Don (T), Virginia Tech | 1961–62 |
| O'Boyle, Henry (B), Notre Dame | 1933 |
| O'Brien, Davey (B), Texas Christian University | 1939–40 |
| O'Brien, Ken (QB), University of California–Davis | 1993 |
| Obst, Henry (G), Syracuse | 1933 |
| Oden, Derrick (LB), Alabama | 1993–95 |
| Olds, Bill (RB), Nebraska | 1976 |
| Oliver, Greg (RB), Trinity (Texas) | 1973–74 |
| Oliver, Hubie (FB), Arizona | 1981–85 |
| O'Neal, Brian (FB), Penn State | 1994 |
| Opperman, Jim (LB), Colorado State | 1975 |
| O'Quinn, John (E), Wake Forest | 1951 |
| Ordway, William (B), North Dakota | 1939 |

| | | | |
|---|---|---|---|
| Oristaglio, Bob (E), Pennsylvania | 1952 | Peters, Scott (C/G), Arizona State | 2002 |
| Ormsbe, Elliott (B), Bradley Tech | 1946 | Peters, Volney (T), Southern California | 1958 |
| Osborn, Mike (LB), Kansas State | 1978 | Pettigrew, Gary (DT), Stanford | 1966–74 |
| Osborne, Richard (TE), Texas A&M | 1976–78 | Philbin, Gerry (DE), Buffalo | 1973 |
| Outlaw, John (DB), Jackson State | 1973–78 | Phillips, Ray (LB), Nebraska | 1978–81 |
| Overmyer, Bill T. (LB), Ashland College | 1972 | Phillips, Ray (DE/LB), North Carolina State† | 1987 |
| Owens, Don (T), Southern Mississippi | 1958–60 | Piasecky, Albert (E), Duke | 1942 |
| Owens, Terrell (WR), Tennessee-Chattanooga | 2004 | Picard, Bob (WR), Washington State | 1973–76 |
| | | Pihos, Pete (E), Indiana | 1947–55 |
| **P** | | Pilconis, Joe (E), Temple | 1934, 1936–37 |
| Pacella, Dave (G/C), Maryland | 1984 | Pinder, Cyril (B), Illinois | 1968–70 |
| Padlow, Max (E), Ohio State | 1935 | Pinkston, Todd (WR), Southern | |
| Pagliei, Joe (B), Clemson | 1959 | Mississippi | 2000–04 |
| Palelei, Lonnie (T/G), University of | | Piro, Henry (E), Syracuse | 1941 |
| Nevada–Las Vegas | 1999 | Pisarcik, Joe (QB), New Mexico State | 1980–84 |
| Palmer, Leslie (B), North Carolina State | 1948 | Pitts, Edwin "Alabama" (B), No College | 1935 |
| Panos, Joe (G), Wisconsin | 1994–97 | Pitts, Mike (DT/DE), Alabama | 1987–92 |
| Papale, Vince (WR), St. Joseph's | 1976–78 | Pivarnick, Joe (G), Notre Dame | 1936 |
| Pape, Oran (B), Iowa | 1933 | Poage, Ray (E), Texas | 1964–65 |
| Parker, Artimus (DB), Southern California | 1974–76 | Pollard, Al (B), West Point | 1951–53 |
| Parker, Rodney (WR), Tennessee State | 1980–81 | Polley, Tom (LB), University of | |
| Parmer, Jim (B), Oklahoma A&M | 1948–56 | Nevada–Las Vegas | 1985 |
| Parry, Josh (FB), San Jose State | 2004 | Pollock, William (B), Penn Military | 1943 |
| Paschka, Gordon (G), Minnesota | 1943 | Porter, Ron (LB), Idaho | 1969–72 |
| Pastorini, Dan (QB), Santa Clara | 1982–83 | Poth, Phil (G), Gonzaga | 1934 |
| Pate, Rupert (G), Wake Forest | 1942 | Powell, Art (B), San Jose State | 1959 |
| Patton, Cliff (G), Texas Christian University | 1946–50 | Powlus, Ron (QB), Notre Dame | 2000 |
| Patterson, Mike (DT), Southern California | 2005 | Preece, Steve (DB), Oregon State | 1970–72 |
| Patton, Jerry (DT), Nebraska | 1974 | Prescott, Harold (E), Hardin-Sim | 1947–49 |
| Payne, Ken (WR), Langston | 1978 | President, Andre (TE), Angelo State (Texas) | 1997 |
| Peaks, Clarence (B), Michigan State | 1957–63 | Priestly, Robert (E), Brown | 1942 |
| Pederson, Doug (QB), Northeast Louisiana | 1999 | Prisco, Nick (B), Rutgers | 1933 |
| Peete, Rodney (QB), Southern California | 1995–98 | Pritchard, Bosh (B), Virginia Military | |
| Pegg, Harold (C), Bucknell | 1940 | Institute | 1942, 1946–51 |
| Pellegrini, Bob (LB), Maryland | 1956, 1958–61 | Pritchett, Stanley (RB), South Carolina | 2000 |
| Penaranda, Jairo (RB), UCLA | 1985 | Puetz, Garry (T), Valparaiso | 1979 |
| Peoples, Woody (G), Grambling | 1978–80 | Pylman, Bob (T), South Dakota State | 1938–39 |
| Perot, Pete (G), Northwestern Louisiana | 1979–84 | Pyne, Jim (C/G), Virginia Tech | 2001 |
| Perrino, Mike (T), Notre Dame† | 1987 | | |
| Perry, Bruce (RB), Maryland | 2004 | **Q** | |
| Perry, William (DT), Clemson | 1993–94 | Quick, Mike (WR), North Carolina State | 1982–90 |
| Peters, Floyd (T), San Francisco State | 1964–69 | Quinlan, Bill (E), Michigan State | 1963 |

# R

| | |
|---|---|
| Rado, George (E), Duquesne | 1937–38 |
| Ragazzo, Phil (T), Wesern Reserve | 1940–41 |
| Ramsey, Herschel (E), Texas Tech | 1938–40, 1945 |
| Ramsey, Knox (G), William & Mary | 1952 |
| Ramsey, Nate (DB), Indiana State | 1963–72 |
| Rash, Lou (CB), Mississippi Valley State | 1984 |
| Raskowski, Leo (T), Ohio State | 1935 |
| Ratliff, Don (DE), Maryland | 1975 |
| Rauch, John (B), Georgia | 1951 |
| Rayburn, Sam (DT), Tulsa | 2003 |
| Raye, Jim (DB), Michigan State | 1969 |
| Reader, Jamie (FB), Akron | 2001 |
| Reagan, Frank (B), Pennsylvania | 1949–51 |
| Reaves, John (QB), Florida | 1972–75 |
| Recher, Dave (C), Iowa | 1965–68 |
| Reed, J.R. (S), South Florida | 2004 |
| Reed, James (LB), California | 1977 |
| Reed, Michael (FB), Washington | 1998 |
| Reed, Taft (B), Jackson State | 1967 |
| Reese, Henry (C/LB), Temple | 1935–39 |
| Reese, Ike (LB), Michigan State | 1998–2004 |
| Reeves, Ken (T), Texas A&M | 1985–89 |
| Reeves, Marion (DB), Clemson | 1974 |
| Reichenbach, Mike (LB), East Stroudsburg | 1984–89 |
| Reichow, Jerry (E), Iowa | 1960 |
| Reid, Alan (RB), Minnesota | 1987 |
| Reid, Mike (S), North Carolina State | 1993–94 |
| Reilly, Kevin (LB), Villanova | 1973–74 |
| Renfro, Leonard (DT), Colorado | 1993–94 |
| Renfro, Will (E), Memphis State | 1961 |
| Repko, Jay (TE), Ursinus† | 1987 |
| Restic, Joe (E), Villanova | 1952 |
| Retzlaff, Pete (E), South Dakota State | 1956–66 |
| Reutt, Ray (E), Virginia Military Institute | 1943 |
| Ricca, Jim (T), Georgetown | 1955–56 |
| Richards, Bobby (E), Louisiana State University | 1962–65 |
| Richardson, Jess (T), Alabama | 1953–61 |
| Richardson, Paul (WR), UCLA | 1993 |
| Riffle, Dick (B), Albright | 1938–40 |
| Riley, Lee (B), Detroit | 1956, 1958–59 |

| | |
|---|---|
| Rimington, Dave (C), Nebraska | 1988–89 |
| Ringo, Jim (C), Syracuse | 1964–67 |
| Rissmiller, Ray (T), Georgia | 1966 |
| Ritchie, Jon (FB), Stanford | 2003–04 |
| Robb, Joe (E), Texas Christian University | 1959–60 |
| Roberts, John (B), Georgia | 1933–34 |
| Robinson, Burle (E), Brigham Young University | 1935 |
| Robinson, Jacque (FB), Washington† | 1987 |
| Robinson, Jerry (LB), UCLA | 1979–84 |
| Robinson, Wayne (LB), Minnesota | 1952–56 |
| Roffler, William (B), Washington State | 1954 |
| Rogalla, John (B), Scranton | 1945 |
| Rogas, Dan (G), Tulane | 1952 |
| Romanowski, Bill (LB), Boston College | 1994–95 |
| Romero, Ray (G), Kansas State | 1951 |
| Roper, Dedrick (LB), Northwood | 2005 |
| Roper, John (LB), Texas A&M | 1993 |
| Rose, Ken (LB), University of Nevada–Las Vegas | 1990–94 |
| Ross, Alvin (FB), Central State (Ohio) † | 1987 |
| Ross, Oliver (T), Iowa State | 1999 |
| Rossovich, Tim (LB), Southern California | 1968–71 |
| Rossum, Allen (CB/KR), Notre Dame | 1998–99 |
| Roton, Herbert (E), Auburn | 1937 |
| Roussel, Tom (LB), Southern Mississippi | 1973 |
| Rowan, Everitt (E), Ohio State | 1933 |
| Rowe, Robert (B), Colgate | 1935 |
| Royals, Mark (P), Appalachian State† | 1987 |
| Rucker, Keith (DT), Ohio Wesleyan | 1996 |
| Rudolph, Joe (G), Wisconsin | 1995 |
| Runager, Max (P), South Carolina | 1979–83, 1989 |
| Runyan, Jon (T), Michigan | 2000 |
| Russell, Booker (FB), Southwest Texas State | 1981 |
| Russell, James (T), Temple | 1936–37 |
| Russell, Laf (B), Northwestern | 1933 |
| Russell, Rusty (T), South Carolina | 1984 |
| Ruzek, Roger (K), Weber State | 1989–93 |
| Ryan, Pat (QB), Tennessee | 1991 |
| Ryan, Rocky (E), Illinois | 1956–58 |
| Ryczek, Paul (C), Virginia† | 1987 |
| Rypien, Mark (QB), Washington State | 1996 |

**S**

| | |
|---|---|
| Sader, Steve (B), No College | 1943 |
| Saidock, Tom (T), Michigan State | 1957 |
| Sampleton, Lawrence (TE), Texas | 1982–84 |
| Samson, Michael (DT), Grambling | 1996 |
| Sanders, John (G), Southern Methodist University | 1943, 1945 |
| Sanders, John (DB), South Dakota | 1977–79 |
| Sanders, Thomas (RB), Texas A&M | 1990–91 |
| Sandifer, Dan (B), Louisiana State University | 1950–51 |
| Sapp, Theron (B), Georgia | 1959–63 |
| Savitsky, George (T), Penn | 1948–49 |
| Saxon, James (FB), San Jose State | 1995 |
| Scarpati, Joe (B), North Carolina State | 1964–69, 1971 |
| Schad, Mike (G), Queen's (Canada) | 1989–93 |
| Schaefer, Don (B), Notre Dame | 1956 |
| Schau, Ryan (T/G), Illinois | 1999–2001 |
| Schmitt, Ted (C), Pittsburgh | 1938–40 |
| Schnelker, Bob (E), Bowling Green | 1953 |
| Schneller, Bill (B), Ole Mississippi | 1940 |
| Schrader, Jim (C), Notre Dame | 1962–64 |
| Schreiber, Adam (G/C), Texas | 1986–88 |
| Schuehle, Jake (B), Rice | 1939 |
| Schultz, Eberle (G), Oregon State | 1940, 1943 |
| Schulz, Jody (LB), East Carolina | 1983–87 |
| Sciarra, John (DB), UCLA | 1978–83 |
| Sciullo, Steve (G), Marshall | 2004 |
| Scott, Clyde (B), Navy/Arkansas | 1949–52 |
| Scott, Gari (WR), Michigan State | 2000–01 |
| Scott, Tom (E), Virginia | 1953–58 |
| Scotti, Ben (B), Maryland | 1962–63 |
| Seals, Leon (DT), Jackson State | 1992 |
| Sears, Vic (T), Oregon State | 1941–53 |
| Seay, Mark (WR), Long Beach State | 1996–97 |
| Sebastian, Mike (B), Pittsburgh | 1935 |
| Selby, Rob (G), Auburn | 1991–94 |
| Shann, Bob (B), Boston College | 1965, 67 |
| Sharkey, Ed (T), Duke | 1954–55 |
| Shaub, Harry (G), Cornell | 1935 |
| Shaw, Rickie (T), North Carolina | 1994 |
| Shaw, Ricky (LB), Oklahoma State | 1989–90 |
| Sheppard, Lito (CB), Florida | 2002 |

| | |
|---|---|
| Sherman, Allie (B), Brooklyn College | 1943–47 |
| Sherman, Heath (RB), Texas A&I | 1989–93 |
| Shires, Marshall (T), Tennessee | 1945 |
| Shonk, John (E), West Virginia | 1941 |
| Short, Jason (LB), Eastern Michigan | 2004 |
| Shuler, Mickey (TE), Penn State | 1990–91 |
| Siano, Mike (WR), Syracuse† | 1987 |
| Sikahema, Vai (WR/PR), Brigham Young University | 1992–93 |
| Simerson, John (C), Purdue | 1957–58 |
| Simmons, Clyde (DE), West Carolina | 1986–93 |
| Simon, Corey (DT), Florida State | 2000–04 |
| Simoneau, Mark (LB), Kansas State | 2005 |
| Sinceno, Kaseem (TE), Syracuse | 1998–99 |
| Sinclair, Michael (DE), Eastern New Mexico | 2002 |
| Singletary, Reggie (DT/G), North Carolina State | 1986–90 |
| Sisemore, Jerry (T), Texas | 1973–84 |
| Sistrunk, Manny (DT), Arkansas AM&N | 1976–79 |
| Skaggs, Jim (G), Washington | 1963–72 |
| Skladany, Leo (E), Pittsburgh | 1949 |
| Skladany, Tom (P), Ohio State | 1983 |
| Slater, Mark (C), Minnesota | 1979–83 |
| Slay, Henry (DT), West Virginia | 1998 |
| Slechta, Jeremy (DT), Nebraska | 2002 |
| Small, Jessie (LB), Eastern Kentucky | 1989–91 |
| Small, Torrance (WR), Alcorn State | 1999–2000 |
| Smalls, Fred (LB), West Virginia† | 1987 |
| Smart, Rod (RB), Western Kentucky | 2001 |
| Smeja, Rudy (E), Michigan | 1946 |
| Smith, Ben (CB/S), Georgia | 1990–93 |
| Smith, Charles (WR), Grambling | 1974–81 |
| Smith, Darrin (LB), Miami (Florida) | 1997 |
| Smith, Daryle (T), Tennessee | 1990–92 |
| Smith, Ed (TE), No College | 1999 |
| Smith, J.D. (T), Rice | 1959–63 |
| Smith, Jack (T), Florida University | 1945 |
| Smith, Jackie (DB), Troy State | 1971 |
| Smith, John (C), Stanford | 1942 |
| Smith, L.J. (TE), Rutgers | 2003 |
| Smith, Milton (E), UCLA | 1945 |
| Smith, Otis (CB), Missouri | 1991–94 |

| | |
|---|---|
| Smith, Phil (WR), San Diego State | 1986 |
| Smith, Ralph (E), Mississippi | 1962–64 |
| Smith, Ray (C), Missouri | 1933 |
| Smith, Rich (C), Ohio State | 1933 |
| Smith, Robert (B), Nebraska | 1956 |
| Smith, Ron (WR), San Diego State | 1981–83 |
| Smith, Steve (T), Michigan | 1971–74 |
| Smith, Troy (WR), East Carolina | 1999 |
| Smothers, Howard (G), Bethune-Cookman | 1995 |
| Smukler, Dave (B), Temple | 1936–39 |
| Snead, Norman (B), Wake Forest | 1964–70 |
| Snyder, Lum (T), Georgia Tech | 1952–55, 1958 |
| Sodaski, John (LB), Villanova | 1972–73 |
| Sokolis, Stan (T), Pennsylvania | 1933 |
| Solomon, Freddie (WR), South Carolina State | 1995–98 |
| Solt, Ron (G), Maryland | 1988–91 |
| Somers, George (T), LaSalle | 1939–40 |
| Spach, Stephen (TE), Fresno State | 2005 |
| Spagnola, John (TE), Yale | 1979–87 |
| Spillers, Ray (T), Arkansas | 1937 |
| Stackpool, John (B), Washington | 1942 |
| Stacy, Siran (RB), Alabama | 1992 |
| Stafford, Dick (E), Texas Tech | 1962–63 |
| Staley, Duce (RB), South Carolina | 1997–2003 |
| Stasica, Leo (B), Colorado | 1941 |
| Steele, Ernie (B), Washington | 1942–48 |
| Steere, Dick (T), Drake | 1951 |
| Steinbock, Laurence (T), St. Thomas | 1933 |
| Steinke, Gil (B), Texas A&I | 1945–48 |
| Stetz, Bill (G), Boston College | 1967 |
| Stevens, Don (B), Illinois | 1952, 1954 |
| Stevens, Matt (S), Appalachian State | 1997–98 |
| Stevens, Pete (C), Temple | 1936 |
| Stevens, Richard (T), Baylor | 1970–74 |
| Steward, Dean (B), Ursinus | 1943 |
| Stewart, Tony (TE), Penn State | 2001–02 |
| Stickel, Walt (T), Pennsylvania | 1950–51 |
| Stockton, Herschel (G), McMurry | 1937–38 |
| Storm, Edward (B), Santa Clara | 1934–35 |
| Strauthers, Tom (DE), Jackson State | 1983–86 |
| Stribling, Bill (E), Mississippi | 1955–57 |

| | |
|---|---|
| Strickland, Donald (DB), Colorado | 2005 |
| Striegel, Bill (G), College of the Pacific | 1959 |
| Stringer, Bob (B), Tulsa | 1952–53 |
| Stuart, Roy (T), Tulsa | 1943 |
| Stubbs, Daniel (DE), Miami (Florida) | 1995 |
| Sturgeon, Cecil (T), North Dakota State | 1941 |
| Sturm, Jerry (C), Illinois | 1972 |
| Suffridge, Bob (G), Tennessee | 1941–45 |
| Sugar, Leo (E), Purdue | 1961 |
| Sullivan, Tom (RB), Miami (Florida) | 1972–77 |
| Supluski, Leonard (E), Dickinson | 1942 |
| Sutton, Joe (B), Temple | 1950–52 |
| Sutton, Mitch (DT), Kansas | 1974–75 |
| Swift, Justin (TE), Kansas State | 1999 |
| Sydner, Jeff (WR/PR), Hawaii | 1992–94 |
| Szafaryn, Len (T), North Carolina | 1957–58 |
| Szymanski, Frank (C), Notre Dame | 1948 |

**T**

| | |
|---|---|
| Talcott, Don (T), Nevada | 1947 |
| Taliaferro, George (B), Indiana | 1955 |
| Tamburello, Ben (C/G), Auburn | 1987–90 |
| Tapeh, Thomas (FB), Minnesota | 2004 |
| Tarasovic, George (E), Louisiana State University | 1963–65 |
| Tarver, John (RB), Colorado | 1975 |
| Tasef, Carl (B), John Carroll | 1961 |
| Tautalatasi, Taivale Jr. (RB), Washington State | 1986–88 |
| Tautolo, Terry (LB), UCLA | 1976–79 |
| Taylor, Bobby (CB), Notre Dame | 1995–2003 |
| Teltschik, John (P), Texas | 1986–90 |
| Thacker, Alvin (B), Morris Harvey | 1941 |
| Thomas, Hollis (DT), Northern Illinois | 1996 |
| Thomas, Johnny (CB), Baylor | 1996 |
| Thomas, Juqua (DE), Oklahoma State | 2005 |
| Thomas, Markus (RB), Eastern Kentucky | 1993 |
| Thomas, Tra (T), Florida State | 1998 |
| Thomas, William (LB), Texas A&M | 1991–99 |
| Thomason, Bobby (B), Virginia Military Institute | 1952–57 |

Thomason, J. "Stumpy" (B), Georgia
  Tech ............................................ 1935–36
Thomason, Jeff (TE), Oregon ...... 2000–02, 2004
Thompson, Broderick (T), Kansas ........ 1993–94
Thompson, Don (E), Richmond ................. 1964
Thompson, Russ (T), Nebraska ................. 1940
Thompson, Tommy (B), Tulsa ............... 1941–42,
  ............................................... 1945–50
Thoms, Art (DE), Syracuse ...................... 1977
Thornton, Richard (B), Missouri
  Mines .......................................... 1933
Thrash, James (WR), Missouri
  Southern ................................... 2001–03
Thrower, Jim (DB), East Texas State ..... 1970–72
Thurbon, Robert (B), Pittsburgh .............. 1943
Timpson, Michael (WR), Penn State .......... 1997
Tinsley, Scott (QB), Southern Cal† .......... 1987
Tom, Mel (DE), San Jose State ............. 1967–73
Tomasetti, Lou (B), Bucknell ............... 1940–41
Toney, Anthony (FB), Texas A&M .......... 1986–90
Torrey, Bob (FB), Penn State ................... 1980
Townsend, Greg (DE), Texas Christian ...... 1994
Tracey, John (E), Texas A&M .................. 1961
Tremble, Greg (DB), Georgia ................... 1995
Tripucka, Frank (B), Notre Dame ............. 1949
Trost, Milton (T), Marquette .................. 1940
Trotter, Jeremiah (LB), Stephen F. ...... 1998–2001,
  Austin ...................................... 2004–05
Troup, Bill (QB), South Carolina .............. 1975
Tupper, Jeff (DE), Oklahoma ................... 1986
Turnbow, Guy (T), Mississippi ............. 1933–34
Turner, Kevin (FB), Alabama ............... 1995–99
Turral, Willie (RB), New Mexico† ............. 1987
Tuten, Rick (P), Florida State ................. 1989
Tyrrell, Joe (G), Temple ....................... 1952

**U**

Ulmer, Michael (DB), Doane College† ........ 1987
Unutoa, Morris (C), Brigham Young
  University ................................. 1996–98
Upersa, Tuufuli (G), Montana ................. 1971
Urevig, Claude (B), North Dakota ............. 1935

**V**

Valentine, Zack (LB), East Carolina ....... 1982–83
Van Brocklin, Norm (QB), Oregon .......... 1958–60
Van Buren, Ebert (B), Louisiana State
  University ................................. 1951–53
Van Buren, Steve (B), Louisiana State
  University ................................. 1944–51
Van Dyke, Alex (WR), Nevada ........... 1999–2000
Van Dyke, Bruce (G), Missouri ................ 1966
Vasys, Arunas (LB), Notre Dame ........... 1966–68
Vick, Roger (RB), Texas A&M .................. 1990
Vincent, Troy (CB), Wisconsin ............ 1996–2003

**W**

Wagner, Steve (S/LB), Wisconsin ........... 1980–81
Wainright, Frank (TE), Northern Colorado .... 1995
Walik, Billy (WR), Villanova ............... 1970–72
Walker, Adam (FB), Pittsburgh ................ 1996
Walker, Corey (RB), Arkansas State ....... 1997–98
Walker, Darwin (DT), Tennessee ............. 2000–
Walker, Herschel (RB), Georgia ............ 1992–94
Wallace, Al (DE/LB), Maryland ............. 1997–99
Walston, Robert (E/K), Georgia ........... 1951–62
Walters, Pete (G), Western Kentucky† ........ 1987
Walters, Stan (T), Syracuse ................ 1975–83
Walton, John (QB), Elizabeth City State ... 1976–79
Ward, Jim (QB), Gettysburg ................ 1971–72
Ware, Matt (CB), UCLA .......................... 2004
Warren, Buist (B), Tennessee .................. 1945
Warren, Chris (RB), Ferrum .................... 2000
Waters, Andre (SS), Cheyney ............... 1984–93
Waters, Mike (FB), San Diego State .......... 1986
Watkins, Foster (B), West Texas State ..... 1940–41
Watkins, Larry (B), Alcorn A&M ........... 1970–72
Watson, Edwin (RB), Purdue .................. 1999
Watson, Tim (SS), Howard ..................... 1997
Watters, Ricky (RB), Notre Dame .......... 1995–97
Wayne, Nate (LB), Mississippi ............. 2003–04
Wear, Robert (C), Penn State .................. 1942
Weatherall, Jim (T), Oklahoma ............. 1955–57
Weaver, Jed (TE), Oregon ...................... 1999
Weber, Chuck (LB), West Chester .......... 1959–61

| | |
|---|---|
| Weedon, Don (G), Texas | 1947 |
| Wegert, Ted (B), No College | 1955–56 |
| Weiner, Albert (B), Muhlenberg | 1934 |
| Weinstock, Isadore (B), Pittsburgh | 1935 |
| Welbourn, John (G/T), California | 1999–2003 |
| Weldon, Casey (QB), Florida State | 1992 |
| Wells, Billy (B), Michigan State | 1958 |
| Wells, Harold (LB), Purdue | 1965–68 |
| Wendlick, Joseph (F), Oregon State | 1940 |
| Wenzel, Jeff (T), Tulane† | 1987 |
| West, Ed (TE), Auburn | 1995–96 |
| West, Hodges (T), Tennessee | 1941 |
| West, Troy (SS), Southern California† | 1987 |
| Westbrook, Brian (RB), Villanova | 2002 |
| Whalen, Jim (E), Boston College | 1971 |
| Wheeler, Mark (DT), Texas A&M | 1999 |
| Whire, John (B), Georgia | 1933 |
| White, Allison (T), Texas Christian University | 1939 |
| White, Reggie (DE/DT), Tennessee | 1985–92 |
| Whiting, Brandon (DT/DE), California | 1998–2003 |
| Whitmore, David (S), Stephen F. Austin | 1995 |
| Whittingham, Fred (LB), California Polytechnic State | 1966, 1971 |
| Wiatrak, John (C), Washington | 1939 |
| Wilburn, Barry (FS), Mississippi | 1995–96 |
| Wilcox, John (T), Oregon | 1960 |
| Wilkes, Reggie (LB), Georgia Tech | 1978–85 |
| Wilkins, Jeff (K), Youngstown State | 1994 |
| Will, Erwin (DT), Dayton | 1965 |
| Willey, Norman (E), Marshall | 1950–57 |
| Williams, Ben (DT), Minnesota | 1999 |
| Williams, Bernard (T), Georgia | 1994 |
| Williams, Bobbie (G), Arkansas | 2000–03 |
| Williams, Boyd (C), Syracuse | 1947 |
| Williams, Byron (WR), University of Texas–Arlington | 1983 |
| Williams, Calvin (WR), Purdue | 1990–96 |
| Williams, Charlie (CB), Jackson State | 1978 |
| Williams, Clyde (T), Georgia Tech | 1935 |
| Williams, Henry (WR/KR), Eastern Carolina | 1989 |
| Williams, Jerry (B), Washington State | 1953–54 |
| Williams, Joel (LB), University of Wisconsin–LaCrosse | 1983–85 |
| Williams, Michael (RB), Mississippi College | 1983–84 |
| Williams, Roger (DB), Grambling | 1973 |
| Williams, Ted (B), Boston College | 1942 |
| Williams, Tex (G), Auburn | 1942 |
| Williams, Tyrone (DE), Wyoming | 1999–2000 |
| Willis, James (LB), Auburn | 1995–98 |
| Wilson, Bill (E), Gonzaga | 1938 |
| Wilson, Brenard (S), Vanderbilt | 1979–86 |
| Wilson, Harry (B), Nebraska | 1967–70 |
| Wilson, Jerry (E), Auburn | 1959–60 |
| Wilson, Osborne (G), Penn | 1933–35 |
| Winfield, Vern (G), Minnesota | 1972–73 |
| Wink, Dean (DT), Yankton | 1967–68 |
| Wirgowski, Dennis (DE), Purdue | 1973 |
| Wistert, Al (T), Michigan | 1943–51 |
| Witherspoon, Derrick (RB), Clemson | 1995–97 |
| Wittenborn, John (G), Southeast Missouri | 1960–62 |
| Wojciechowicz, Alex (C), Fordham | 1946–50 |
| Wolfe, Hugh (B), West Texas Teachers College | 1940 |
| Woltman, Clem (T), Purdue | 1938–40 |
| Woodard, Marc (LB), Mississippi State | 1994–96 |
| Woodeshick, Tom (B), West Virginia | 1963–71 |
| Woodruff, Lee (B), Mississippi | 1933 |
| Woodruff, Tony (WR), Fresno State | 1982–84 |
| Woodson, Sean (S), Jackson State | 1998 |
| Worden, Neil (B), Notre Dame | 1954, 1957 |
| Woulfe, Mike (LB), Colorado | 1962 |
| Wright, Gordon (G), Delaware State | 1967 |
| Wright, Sylvester (LB), Kansas | 1995–96 |
| Wukits, Al (C), Duquesne | 1943 |
| Wyatt, Antwuan (WR), Bethune-Cookman | 1997 |
| Wydo, Frank (T), Duquesne/Cornell | 1952–57 |
| Wyhonic, John (G), Alabama | 1946–47 |
| Wynn, Dexter (CB), Colorado State | 2004– |
| Wynn, William (DE), Tennessee State | 1973–76 |

**Y**

| | |
|---|---|
| Young, Adrian (LB), Southern California | 1968–72 |
| Young, Charle (TE), Southern California | 1973–76 |
| Young, Glen (WR), Mississippi State | 1983 |
| Young, Michael (WR), UCLA | 1993 |
| Young, Roynell (CB), Alcorn State | 1980–88 |
| Youngelman, Sid (T), Alabama | 1956–58 |
| Yovicsin, John (E), Gettysburg | 1944 |

**Z**

| | |
|---|---|
| Zabel, Steve (E/LB), Oklahoma | 1970–74 |
| Zandofsky, Mike (G), Washington | 1997 |
| Zendejas, Luis (K), Arizona State | 1988–89 |
| Ziegler, Frank (B), Georgia Tech | 1949–53 |
| Zilly, John (E), Notre Dame | 1952 |
| Zimmerman, Don (WR), Northeast Louisiana | 1972–76 |
| Zimmerman, Roy (B), San Jose State | 1942–46 |
| Zizak, Vince (T), Villanova | 1934–37 |
| Zomalt, Eric (SS), California | 1994–96 |
| Zordich, Michael (SS), Penn State | 1994–98 |
| Zyntell, James (G), Holy Cross | 1933–35 |

# Notes

### The Yellow Jackets Buzz

"Every move Homan makes is colorful. ..." Daly, Dan, and Bob O' Connell, *The Pro Football Chronicle*. New York: MacMillan Publishing Co., 1990.

"A spectacle of joyful exuberance not witnessed in this..." Daly, Dan, and Bob O' Connell, *The Pro Football Chronicle*. New York: MacMillan Publishing Co., 1990.

### A Jailbird and a Star: Alabama Pitts

"Unfortunately in every way. The Association president was wrong. ..." Daly, Dan, and Bob O' Connell, *The Pro Football Chronicle*. New York: MacMillan Publishing Co., 1990.

"You see, where I was, we didn't get out much at night..." Daly, Dan, and Bob O' Connell, *The Pro Football Chronicle*. New York: MacMillan Publishing Co., 1990.

"Pitts has a bright future," Bell told reporters. ..." Daly, Dan, and Bob O' Connell, *The Pro Football Chronicle*. New York: MacMillan Publishing Co., 1990.

### Bell's Vision

"A dark cloud passed over the sky somewhere north of Manayunk. ..." Daly, Dan, and Bob O' Connell, *The Pro Football Chronicle*. New York: MacMillan Publishing Co., 1990.

"One of the strongest feuds that the league has ever known." Daly, Dan, and Bob O' Connell, *The Pro Football Chronicle*. New York: MacMillan Publishing Co., 1990.

## Trading Teams
"Extremely happy to come to Philadelphia. ..." Thompson, Alexis, and Donald
  R. Campbell. *Sunday Warriors,* Philadelphia: Quantum Leap Publisher, 1994.

## A Football Innovator: Greasy Neale
"My first love was baseball and my consuming ambition..." Neale, Earle
  "Greasy." *Colliers*, November 17, 1951.
"Yale or no Yale, you fellows want to call me Greasy, go ahead. ..." Neale, Earle
  "Greasy." *Colliers*, November 17, 1951.
"We had 68 books that we took into..." Neale, Earle "Greasy." *Pro Football
  Digest,* April–May 1968.
"I'm terribly superstitious and wear the same suit..." Neale, Earle "Greasy."
  *Colliers*, November 17, 1951.
"It was a complete surprise. ..." Neale, Earle "Greasy." *Pro Football Digest*,
  April–May 1968.

## The Steagles Take the Stage
"Don't you think (two teams)'d be able to come up..." Daly, Dan, and Bob
  O' Connell, *The Pro Football Chronicle*. New York: MacMillan Publishing Co.,
  1990.

## "Wham Bam" Van Buren Takes the Eagles to the Top
"Thorpe was a bigger man than Van Buren..." Smith, Ron, et al. *The Sporting
  News Selects...Football's 100 Greatest Players,* St. Louis: Sporting News
  Publishing Company, July 1999.
"I wanted to get tackled in that game..." http://www.philadelphiaeagles.com.
"He was out of this world that day. ..." http://www.philadelphiaeagles.com.
"I used to take maybe six shots (painkilling injections) each half. ..."
  http://www.philadelphiaeagles.com.
"If I could have run long, I could have been better. ..."
  http://www.philadelphiaeagles.com.

## Titletown I
"I don't want to work all year for one big..." Carroll, Bob, and the Pro Football
  Hall of Fame. "Snowbirds: The 1948 Philadelphia Eagles," Pro Football
  Researchers Association,
  http://www.footballresearch.com/articles/frpage.cfm?topic=phila48.

## Titletown II

"I think we belong with the best teams ever. ..."
   http://www.philadelphiaeagles.com.

## Concrete Charlie: The Incomparable Chuck Bednarik

"How we survived, I don't know. ..." Flatter, Ron. "Sixty-Minute Man,"
   ESPN.com, http://espn.go.com/classic/biography/s/Bednarik_Chuck.html.
"I admired him so much. ..." "Chat Transcript with Chuck Bednarik," Pro
   Football Hall of Fame,
   http://www.profootballhof.com/history/release.jsp?release_id=734.
"I bought a brand-new house for $14,500..." "Chat Transcript with Chuck
   Bednarik," Pro Football Hall of Fame,
   http://www.profootballhof.com/history/release.jsp?release_id=734.
"He was doing a down-and-in pattern..." "Chat Transcript with Chuck
   Bednarik," Pro Football Hall of Fame,
   http://www.profootballhof.com/history/release.jsp?release_id=734.
"That game without a doubt was the greatest..." "Chat Transcript with Chuck
   Bednarik," Pro Football Hall of Fame,
   http://www.profootballhof.com/history/release.jsp?release_id=734.
"I always played with a certain amount of cockiness. ..." Smith, Don. *Pro*
   magazine, 1980.

## Champions

"That game without a doubt was the greatest game I ever had." "Chat
   Transcript with Chuck Bednarik," Pro Football Hall of Fame,
   http://www.profootballhof.com/history/release.jsp?release_id=734.

## Tommy McDonald: A Showman and a Star

"Most of the time, Tommy doesn't have to..."
   http://www.philadelphiaeagles.com.
"You just throw the ball." http://www.philadelphiaeagles.com.
"He just lives in another world." http://www.philadelphiaeagles.com.
"I used to have to shut him up." http://www.philadelphiaeagles.com.

## The Abyss

"I let out all my anger of the whole year..." Daly, Dan, and Bob O' Connell, *The*
   *Pro Football Chronicle.* New York: MacMillan Publishing Co., 1990.

## Promises of a Super Bowl: The Arrival of Dick Vermeil

"I don't want to put our other coaches down…" Rambeck, Richard. *Philadelphia Eagles*, Mankato, Minnesota: Creative Education, Inc., 1990.

"In five years, the Eagles will be Super Bowl material." Rambeck, Richard. *Philadelphia Eagles*, Mankato, Minnesota: Creative Education, Inc., 1990.

## The Polish Rifle Comes to Philly: Ron Jaworski Joins the Eagles

"When I first got to Philadelphia…" Rothhaus, James. The Philadelphia Eagles, Mankato, Minnesota: Creative Education, Inc., 1986.

"I thought he was crazy. …" Rambeck, Richard. *Philadelphia Eagles*, Mankato, Minnesota: Creative Education, Inc., 1990.

"My dad worked in a lumber yard…" Ronjawarski.com, http://www.ronjaworski.com/about_rj.php.

"The summer before my senior year…" Ronjawarski.com, http://www.ronjaworski.com/about_rj.php.

"He didn't come up with Jaws…" Ronjawarski.com, http://www.ronjaworski.com/about_rj.php.

## The Road to the Super Bowl

"We hear that leather pop…" Rambeck, Richard. *Philadelphia Eagles*, Mankato, Minnesota: Creative Education, Inc., 1990.

"The NFC championship game was our Super Bowl. …" http://www.philadelphiaeagles.com.

## Burnout

"When we went to the Super Bowl…" Rothhaus, James. *The Philadelphia Eagles*, Mankato, Minnesota: Creative Education, Inc., 1986.

## "Bud-dee, Bud-dee"

"Any Eagles fan will tell you…" http://www.philadelphiaeagles.com.

## A Championship Pedigree

"Everyone who works with him and plays for him…" Philadelphia Eagles media guide.

"We are excited but yet we have another game left. …" Donovanmcnabb.com.

## When McNabb Touched Down

"People ask for my autograph..." Philadelphia Eagles media guide.

"I thought he was probably best wired..." Donovanmcnabb.com.

"A number of commentators will say..." NFL.com. Wire reports, November 5, 2005.

"He's always carried himself with class. ..." Donovanmcnabb.com.

"I believe Donovan McNabb is one of the best..." Donovanmcnabb.com.

"I play this game to be the best. ..." Donovanmcnabb.com.

## Missing Line Found?

"I was looking forward to the playoffs..." NFL.com. Wire reports, November 5, 2005.

"The good quarterbacks are probably like fighter pilots. ..." Philadelphia Eagles media guide.

## As the World Turns

"I choose to be amused because I have a job to do. ..." Donovanmcnabb.com.

"I made the decision and went with it..." http://www.philadelphiaeagles.com.